PERFORMANCE PLANNING AND REVIEW

MAKING EMPLOYEE APPRAISALS WORK
2ND EDITION

Richard Rudman

ALLEN&UNWIN

First published in 1995

Copyright © Richard Rudman

This edition first published 2003

83 Alexander Street,
Crows Nest NSW 2065 Australia
Phone: (61 2) 8425 0100
Fax: (61 2) 9906 2218
E-mail: info@allenandunwin.com
Web: www.allenandunwin.com

National Library of Australia
Cataloguing-in-Publication entry:

Rudman, R.S. (Richard Stanley), 1948– .
Performance planning and review : making employee
appraisals work.

2nd ed.
Bibliography.
Includes index.
ISBN 1 74114 103 6.

1. Employees - Rating of. 2. Personnel management.
I. Title

658.3125

Set in 10.5/13 pt Sabon by Midland Typesetters
Printed by CMO Image Printing, Singapore

10 9 8 7 6 5 4 3 2 1

CONTENTS

1 THE CHALLENGE OF PERFORMANCE MANAGEMENT   **1**
* Grasping the challenge   2
* Adapting to change   5

2 PERFORMANCE AND PERFORMANCE MANAGEMENT   **7**
* Performance management and the organisation   8
* Performance management and the manager   10
* Performance management and the job   13
* Performance management and the work team   15
* Performance management and the 'new' employee   16
* Panacea or disease?   20

3 DEVELOPING A PERFORMANCE MANAGEMENT SYSTEM   **22**
* Deciding on objectives   24
* Conflicts   26
* Effective performance management systems   31
* Overcoming objections   40

4 PLANNING PERFORMANCE   **45**
* Performance planning and the job description   45
* Writing job descriptions   47
* Job descriptions as performance contracts   49
* Standards, targets, objectives and measures   51
* Principles and benefits of performance measurement   54
* Setting targets   55
* Targets for managers   60

5 REVIEWING PERFORMANCE   **66**
* What performance do we review?   67
* How do we review performance?   68
* Performance review methods   69
* Comparison or ranking methods   70
* Standards-based reviews   73

- Results-oriented reviews   88
- Competency-based methods   93
- Problems of error in performance reviews   98
- Who should do the performance review?   101
- Training for reviewers   113

6 DISCUSSING PERFORMANCE   **115**
- Preparing for the discussion   119
- Arrangements for the performance discussion   120
- The structure of the discussion   122
- Communication skills   126
- A model format   133

7 DEVELOPING PERFORMANCE   **144**
- The manager's role   145
- Training and learning   147
- The manager as coach   153
- Coaching for performance improvement   158
- The performance development discussion   159
- Handling performance problems   166
- Career development   169

8 REWARDING PERFORMANCE   **173**
- Performance and rewards   175
- Equity and expectancy   177
- Linking pay to performance review   178
- Effective performance pay schemes   181
- Types of performance pay   182
- Paying for performance   184

9 PERFORMANCE PLANNING AND REVIEW FOR TEAMS   **193**
- Different kinds of teams   196
- Whose performance?   197
- Teams and individuals   198
- What performance?   200
- Who reviews team performance?   204
- Rewarding team performance   207

References   211
Index   216

CHAPTER 1

THE CHALLENGE OF PERFORMANCE MANAGEMENT

Few people look forward to the annual performance appraisal interview. Managers don't like being put in the role of judge. Employees don't like being evaluated. So performance appraisals get done because the system requires it. We often hear complaints like this—especially where employees' performance is being assessed in isolation from the organisation's business and operating objectives. Or where performance appraisal is a once-a-year event which neither managers nor employees see as a positive contributor to working relationships or work performance.

Complaints like this lead to calls for performance appraisal to be abandoned or abolished. For example, the grand old man of quality management, W. Edwards Deming, once described performance appraisal as a 'deadly disease' (Deming 1986) and Professor Clive Fletcher suggested in the early 1990s that appraisal might be 'an idea whose time had gone' (Fletcher 1993a).

The critics have some things in common. First, they assert that performance appraisals fail to achieve their stated objectives and thus serve no useful purpose. But they don't examine why this is so. Second, they condemn the performance appraisal practices of some organisations as succeeding only in demoralising and demotivating their employees, and then generalise from these examples. Next, they cite examples of organisations which have done away with appraisals—but then gone on to replace them with performance planning or employee development planning or other processes that mirror the practices of many organisations that are firmly committed to their performance management systems. Fourth, the critics find it difficult to suggest how organisations might direct and assess what their employees do without using some form of performance management. It's easy to take the negative case if you don't have to suggest an alternative.

On the other side of the argument are people like Tom Peters—one of the authors of the ground-breaking *In Search of Excellence*—who argues that 'dynamic employee evaluation is more critical than ever' in a world where both organisations and work are changing rapidly (Peters 1994). It seems that most organisations, and many of their employees, agree. Surveys all over the world show that most organisations use some form of performance appraisal. It might be true that appraisals work best in cultures—whether societal or organisational—where people are comfortable with open discussion and where it is acceptable for managers and their employees to give and receive feedback. But cultural differences are a poor excuse for avoiding the review and discussion of performance: organisations and managers should ensure that all their practices and behaviours are appropriate and sensitive to the needs and aspirations of their people.

Performance appraisals might add to the pressures on managers' time, and they might be a source of disappointment or discontent for employees who feel they are treated unreasonably. Yet a British study reveals that, for a majority of more than 35 000 people it surveyed, the annual appraisal encourages employees to feel valued, engenders a sense of personal and career development and increases organisational commitment (Strebler et al. 2001). In many aspects of their working lives, employees who receive appraisals are significantly more satisfied and feel significantly more positive than those who do not.

Other UK research suggests that performance reviews have an even more important role: it seems that employees who receive appraisals are not only more positive about their jobs but more competent at them as well (Borrill et al. 2001). A study of 61 hospitals led by Professor Michael West of the Aston Business School showed that the extent and sophistication of appraisal systems was closely related to lower patient mortality rates. Of the various human resources practices tested by the researchers, appraisal was found to have the strongest relationship with patient mortality. Most organisations might not be in the business of saving lives, but they should appreciate the significance of this research-based linkage between being appraised and performing well.

GRASPING THE CHALLENGE

Managing people and performance has always been a challenge for organisations and managers. Inevitably, the first performance appraisal was made soon after the first employer hired the first employee. Ever since, employers have been making judgments about their employees: Are they doing what we want them to? How does this person's performance compare with others? What are this employee's strengths? What training does that employee need? Shall we give this employee a salary increase? Or promote that employee?

Managers have always found performance appraisal challenging. Most of us—mistakenly, as it happens—think we are reasonably good judges of other people. Yet we seem to find it difficult to assess our employees' work, to communicate those assessments to the people concerned, and so achieve the changes in attitudes and behaviour that will lead to improved performance. Perhaps the problem is the frequent use of the term performance *appraisal* which—for me, anyway—implies being judgmental. Perhaps managers are unsure about the information and skills they use to make and communicate their assessments; perhaps employees are reluctant to accept these assessments if they could adversely affect their salaries or careers.

Perhaps neither managers nor employees see performance appraisal as worthwhile. For managers, it might be just another time-consuming, bureaucratic requirement; for employees, it might be seen as another example of top-down management decision-making. Perhaps neither managers nor employees see the performance appraisal system as a tool for managing and improving performance. Indeed, it might be worth asking whether the information collected on appraisal forms is ever actually used for management decision-making—or simply filed away in the human resources department.

Internationally, according to one survey, more than 80 per cent of all workplaces subject their employees to some form of regular performance appraisal—yet only about 5 per cent are satisfied with the results. Here are some changes that might help the others to improve this situation.

Try a new name

Performance appraisal should emphasise *planning* as much as *review*. So why not use those words? The new name would be a constant reminder of this dual function. Accordingly, this book uses *performance planning and review* in preference to 'performance appraisal' to describe the process of setting employees' work plans and targets and reviewing their performance. A change in name might also help to shift the emphasis away from 'judgment' and 'appraisal' towards a recognition that sensible assessments of another person's performance are not really possible if you don't know what that person set out to achieve. Nor can an employee be expected to achieve performance standards or targets without knowing what they are from the outset.

Focus on performance

Performance planning and review should focus on performance. Performance appraisal systems that gather data for decisions about remuneration, training, promotion and career development are probably trying to do too much: they might end up doing none of these things very well. The focus on performance should be just that, and not extend to consideration of the employee's personality or other characteristics. In addition, the key question to ask is 'How well is this employee performing in terms of the plans and targets we agreed on?'—not 'How well is the employee performing in comparison with others in the work group?'

Make it fit

The performance planning and review process must suit the environment and culture of the organisation. This requires more than lip service to the latest business buzz words and management fads: it means the organisation has to be sure that what it does in practice is consistent with the promise it makes. Does an organisation risk its credibility if it preaches employee empowerment but makes appraisals compulsory? Is a 'one-size-fits-all' appraisal system consistent with a policy of encouraging diversity? How do you reconcile a team-based approach to working with a system of individual performance reviews?

In addition, the people who have to make performance planning and review work effectively—that is, all the managers and all their employees—must be given the skills and confidence to use its processes as part of their normal management and working roles.

Take a total approach

Simply changing the name and emphasis will not be enough unless performance planning and review is central to the organisation's total approach to performance management. It might have been appropriate once to describe performance appraisal as 'simply an attempt to think clearly about each person's current performance and future prospects against the background of the total work situation' (Mayfield 1960). Back then, of course, the world was a much more straightforward place. Today, organisations must pay close attention to the management of performance as they struggle to be competitive in constantly changing markets and circumstances. The structure of organisations, the nature of the work they do and the people they employ have all changed dramatically over the past few decades—and so has the nature of the performance that must be managed.

Performance planning and review should be part of a total approach to performance management. Employees must be able to see how their work contributes to the achievement of the organisation's overall goals;

how they are managed should encourage them to want to make a better contribution; they should be helped to develop their skills and talents so that they can improve their contributions; and those contributions should be recognised and rewarded in ways that make employees feel good about themselves, their jobs and their employer.

Thus, an interview that takes place on one day of the year is much less important than what happens on all the other days. And on all those days when there is no performance appraisal scheduled, employees' performance cannot be left to happen by itself. Just like people, performance must be managed.

ADAPTING TO CHANGE

Performance appraisal's critics voice a wide range of objections. Here's a selection of them.

- The vertical hierarchy implied by performance appraisal is not the typical structure of today's organisations.
- Organisations no longer rely on a 'command-control' model of management.
- Jobs are now less tightly defined and less rigidly specified.
- People's roles are constantly changing and cannot be precisely defined in advance.
- More and more workers are engaged on a contingent or temporary basis, often for short-term or project roles where the expected performance outcomes are defined in advance.
- Customers and clients have as much influence on work demands and standards as do managers and corporate plans.
- Managers should act as leaders and facilitators rather than directors.
- The workplace has become more 'collective' or 'feminine', with a greater emphasis on social skills and consensus-building.
- Teams rather than individuals are responsible for producing work.
- Employee performance depends more on the organisation's systems than on individual efforts.
- Organisation charts cannot show the influence networks that have replaced one-on-one management–subordinate relationships.
- Self-management is the key to success, not doing what others tell you.
- Appraisals are, inescapably, biased and inconsistent: they do more harm than good.

Undoubtedly, some of these trends and developments are found in some organisations today. Certainly, many organisations have flatter hierarchies, leaner structures with fewer middle managers and wider spans of control, more flexible employment and work practices, more open communication and consultative management styles and team-based work systems. But it is an exaggeration, surely, to assert that all organisations have taken on these 'new' characteristics. And, even if they had, what the critics fail to explain is how these trends and developments invalidate either the concept of performance management or the process of planning and reviewing performance.

All these changes have an impact on traditional approaches to performance appraisal. Often, however, the appropriate response is a change in emphasis or style: abandoning any form of performance planning and review would be, at best, an over-reaction. It would not help the organisation, or its managers, or its employees. As we see in Chapter 2, every organisation needs some system or framework for determining what has to be done, how, to what standards or levels and by whom.

The shape and style of that system or framework is the subject of this book. Each organisation's choices should be made only after it has asked—and answered—some searching questions. What are the aims of performance planning and review? How can we make it work for us in a rapidly changing environment? Who 'owns' the system? Who makes the performance plans? Who contributes to the reviews? What criteria do they use?

What you will find throughout this book is advice on how to adapt your approach to performance planning and review to meet the new challenges and suit the new realities. Here are a few key trends that are discussed in later chapters.

- Closer linking of organisational, departmental, team and individual objectives within an overall performance management framework (see Chapter 2).
- Greater emphasis on performance and personal development, so that performance reviews are concerned less with appraisal and rating than with future improvement and development (see Chapter 7).
- Increasing use of competency-based assessments, which focus on the abilities employees need to respond to changing demands and environments (see Chapter 5).
- Using multi-rater methods such as 360-degree feedback to widen the pool of information available for performance planning and review (see Chapter 5).
- Development of team-based approaches to planning, reviewing and rewarding the performance of work groups (see Chapter 9).

CHAPTER 2

PERFORMANCE AND PERFORMANCE MANAGEMENT

Performance has become a business buzz word. That's not a bad thing, especially if it works to remind us that organisations exist for a purpose. They're established to do things and to achieve results—and that applies to public service and not-for-profit organisations as much as to profit-motivated commercial firms.

Organisations use many different approaches in the quest for a high-performance workplace. Manufacturers turn to lean production and just-in-time methods; small businesses use flexible specialisation to harness networks; production and service organisations put the focus on total quality or continuous improvement; team-working is more and more common; corporations and processes are re-engineered—and so on. What everyone realises, sooner or later, is that the organisation's performance is only partly dependent on its technology, processes and systems. What is more important is the performance of its employees—and so the management of employees' performance is a principal contributor to organisational success.

But what does *performance* actually mean? It can be defined very simply as *focused behaviour* or *purposeful work*. In other words, jobs exist to achieve specific and defined results, and people are employed to do those jobs because the organisation wants to achieve those results. Thus, *performance* is what we need from employees if organisations are to achieve their business objectives.

However, *job performance* is different from mere *work activity*. People can spend their days writing reports, going to meetings, operating machines, driving buses or talking with colleagues—but those are *work activities*. They must be put in a context of what the organisation wants its employees to do, and how well, before we can assess whether work activities are contributing to effective performance, for either the individual or the organisation. The manager's role is to help employees focus their behaviour—in other words, to convert their *activity* into *performance*. That conversion is not very difficult, so long as managers

7

remember that employees are essentially looking for answers to four simple questions.

- What do you want me to do?
- How well do you want me to do it?
- How well am I doing? What do you think of my performance?
- How will I be rewarded for my contribution?

To answer these questions, the organisation must be able to:

- describe what work it wants people to do;
- establish performance levels and standards for the work;
- set performance goals or targets for individual employees or work teams;
- provide information and feedback to employees on their performance;
- offer employees appropriate rewards and remuneration.

An organisation that can consistently answer these questions for its employees will have, at least, the foundations of an effective performance management system. It will probably also have a team of effective performance managers. Unfortunately, the definition of management as 'achieving results through people' became unpopular for a while because it was seen as too simplistic for complex and sophisticated organisations. The focus for managers seemed to shift to the technical content of the work their staff were doing. Today, in a world of rapid change, new technologies, flatter hierarchies and networked organisations, 'achieving results through people' is once again the manager's main role—and the manager's key skill as well. Using performance planning and review techniques within an organisation-wide system of performance management makes it easier for managers to play that role effectively.

PERFORMANCE MANAGEMENT AND THE ORGANISATION

Like many modern management ideas, *performance management* originated in the United States. From there the concept has spread widely, as organisations look for systems or structures to reinforce their new-found focus on performance. In some cases, performance management has been just a new name for 'Management by Objectives' (MBO), where individual employees are assigned performance targets cascaded down from departmental or organisational goals. Others have used performance management to try to breathe new life into old-style performance appraisal systems which refused to work. Others see performance management as a mechanism for making performance-related pay decisions. Still others see it as a creature of 'new right' management and just another way to exploit workers.

More positively, performance management may be seen as a total approach to managing people and performance. It involves setting performance aims and expectations for the organisation as a whole, for each business or operating unit within the organisation, and for work groups and individual employees. This framework of performance management is now generally regarded as essential to the success of any system of performance planning and review.

Performance management

- The process of identifying, evaluating and developing the work performance of employees in the organisation, so that organisational goals and objectives are more effectively achieved, while at the same time benefiting employees in terms of recognition, receiving feedback, catering for work needs and offering career guidance (Lansbury 1988).
- A process or set of processes for establishing shared understanding about what is to be achieved, and of managing and developing people in a way which increases the probability that it will be achieved in the short and longer term (Armstrong 1992).

Originally, performance management was seen as an approach to directing and controlling people's performance by systematically linking job requirements, job behaviours and job rewards in ways that recognised both individual needs and organisational objectives (Conole & O'Neill 1985). Today, the emphasis is on integration and agreement rather than direction and control. Thus, a performance management system will probably start with a description of the organisation's mission, goals and values. Corporate and divisional objectives which support that mission are then formulated, and translated into goals for managers, work teams and individual employees.

In the past, this exercise would have been undertaken by top management. Subsequently, the strategies and plans would have been cascaded down through the organisation so that all employees could see how their roles fitted into the larger picture. Today, it is more likely that individual employees and work groups at all levels will be involved in setting their goals. Most top managers now understand the need to share the organisation's aims and objectives widely, to provide information about performance and results, to seek comment and feedback, to get ideas and suggestions—indeed, to make people feel part of their enterprise. Performance management systems can be an effective means for such communication.

The performance management concept goes beyond the traditional straight-line approach to linking organisational objectives and individual behaviour and becomes a process for planning, monitoring, reviewing, rewarding and developing performance through systematically linking employees' needs and organisational objectives. *Performance appraisal* could be seen as a means of control; *performance management* is more a process for integrating the management of the organisation with the management of its people. It is also a way of integrating human resources policies and programs which might otherwise operate largely in isolation (see Figure 2.1).

PERFORMANCE MANAGEMENT AND THE MANAGER

The usual focus of performance appraisal is an annual appraisal interview between managers and their subordinates. Few people look forward to this once-a-year meeting. In contrast, the performance management approach says that what happens on the day of the performance planning and review discussion can only be truly effective if people and their performance are properly managed during the whole year. In other words, employees' performance throughout the year should not be left to chance. Employees need to understand their jobs and what is expected of them— the *performance plan*—and should be encouraged and assisted by their managers throughout the year with feedback and coaching to fulfil the plan. In this way, the *performance review* becomes a summary discussion which holds no surprises for either the employee or the manager.

Many managers try to avoid this summary discussion by claiming that they are constantly planning and reviewing the performance of their employees on a day-by-day basis. They argue that the ideal form of performance appraisal is frequent communication and feedback on the job. But they forget that this day-to-day contact involves mainly the particular problems and challenges of the moment: its focus is the short term. In any case, continuing communication between managers and their staff will be more effective if it takes place in the context of agreed performance plans and objectives. In addition, new organisational systems and structures, and the impact of such changes as globalisation mean that many managers are now geographically or functionally distant

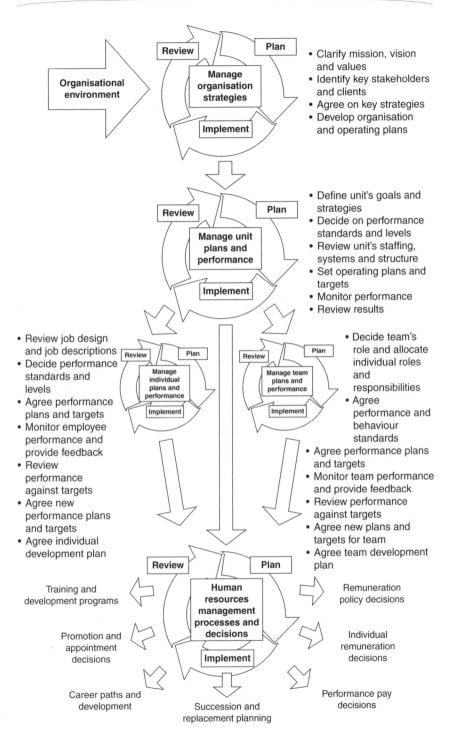

FIGURE 2.1 A PERFORMANCE MANAGEMENT PROCESS

from their direct reports on a day-to-day basis. For them, a regular performance planning and review session provides a necessary operating framework and develops mutual confidence that the right things are being done in the right way.

Performance appraisal systems often fail because managers approach the discussion of employees' performance as a once-a-year event. During the time the interview takes, the manager tries to be supportive and helpful and encourages the employee to share ideas. But this behaviour often does not persist beyond the interview. Ironically, many managers seem to be better at performance management than they are at performance appraisal. After all, they spend much of their time managing the performance of their staff: they have expectations of what employees should do; they communicate those expectations to the employees; they monitor their performance; they let them know when things go wrong; they praise them for good work or extra effort; they assess their employees' skills and performance and value to the organisation, and recommend or take actions based on those opinions. In other words, managers use many of the elements of the performance management process on a day-to-day basis. And they recognise the value of the process, if only because their own prospects and rewards depend on how well they are seen to manage the performance of their people.

Why, then, do managers dislike formal systems of performance planning and review? Why do they consider performance management to be a 'requirement' that is somehow separate and remote from their 'real' job responsibilities?

One answer is that many managers see the performance management system as the creature of the human resources department. Indeed, many managers admit that they conduct performance appraisals only because the organisation requires them to do so. In other words, people who are managing performance effectively on a day-to-day basis do not—or are not willing to—'own' a formal system of performance management. One reason for this might be that managers don't believe they have the skills and knowledge they need to manage performance effectively. Perhaps the agendas for manager training programs need to be shifted from the content of 'management' to the skills of 'managing'.

Another reason is that few organisations clearly and overtly recognise that the manager's key role is to manage the performance of others. Performance management systems can only work effectively when they become part of 'the way we manage around here'. Indeed, managers should be held directly accountable for the effective performance management of their staff—and this accountability should form part of their own performance plans, reviews and rewards.

PERFORMANCE MANAGEMENT AND THE JOB

Despite all the changes to work and the workplace—perhaps even because of them—each of us needs to know just what it is we're expected to do. In other words, every job must have a clear framework and focus. Basically, a job is just a collection of work activities—tasks which the organisation needs to have done so that it can fulfil its role and achieve its objectives. Yet a job is much more than that. For most people, it is a primary source of social identity. Have you noticed how, after finding out a person's name, the first question we ask is 'What do you do?' We're really asking 'What's your job?' In this way, the job is an important source of identity and self-esteem; it is also a source of personal satisfaction if people consider their jobs to be significant and worthwhile.

In the past, especially in large organisations, people were engaged to carry out the tasks and duties of a particular job. The French coined the term *bureaucrat* for a person who held an office—*bureau* translates as 'office'—and was responsible for undertaking its assigned duties according to official rules and procedures. Bureaucracy emphasised administration rather than management, inputs rather than outcomes, and activity rather than achievement. The focus of today's organisation is rather different.

Organisations need to arrange their work activities—that is, design jobs—in ways that suit the technologies they use, the environments they operate in, the organisational style and culture, and their business or service aims and objectives. Regrettably, few organisations pay close attention to job design. Others argue that the design of individual jobs is less important now that team-working and flexible employment arrangements are in vogue. This argument can be countered in three ways.

- Most employees don't work in teams or flexible arrangements—and won't do so for the foreseeable future.
- Work activities are carried out mainly by individuals—even though they might interact cooperatively with others while carrying out their assigned activities—and this is unlikely to change. After all, even the most effective team workers (the members of a sports team, for example) are selected because they have the individual skills and talents needed for the unique requirements of different positions in the game. Team members might be able to play in more than one position, and from time to time will have to play as a group 'on attack' or 'in defence' rather than as individuals, yet the game and the team are designed, and the game plan and the

team membership decided, in order to recognise the needs of different roles.

- The introduction of flexible working styles and contingent forms of employment make it more, not less, important to pay attention to job design. We can no longer assume, as we could in the past, that there will be a basic similarity in the structure and organisation of most jobs, so we need to be sure that work activities are allocated and organised in ways that enhance the opportunities for employee achievement and satisfaction.

In a sense, the individual job—the way in which a particular set of work activities is organised and set in a network of relationships with other jobs and people—is the fundamental building block of the organisation. At the same time, the one-on-one relationships between job holders and their managers are the key to communication within the organisation and the basis for sound performance management.

Any organisation can develop a systematic approach to job design, using the research-based principles outlined below. But you need more than a checklist for drawing up job descriptions: you need a total approach to analysing and organising work activity that links the business and operating needs and objectives of the organisation with the performance and development needs and objectives of employees. That is a very good first step on the road to effective performance management.

Four approaches to job design

Turner and Lawrence (1965) say that motivation in a job comes from:
- *variety* in work activities
- *autonomy* in determining what methods of work to use
- *interaction with others* in carrying out the work and at other times
- *knowledge and skills* sufficient to do the work
- *responsibility* for problem-solving and other decisions.

Cooper (1973) says employees' motivation will be improved by:
- *variety* in tasks, surroundings, and the people available for interaction
- *discretion* in choosing how to do the work and in selecting how to solve problems
- *goals* which are clear but sufficiently challenging
- *contribution* of a kind and at a level that enables employees to see that their work matters.

Frederick Herzberg (1974) lists eight ingredients of job enrichment:
- direct *feedback*
- a *client* relationship
- a *learning* function
- *opportunity* for the employee to schedule the work
- unique *expertise*
- *control* over resources
- *direct communication*
- *personal accountability*.

Hackman and Oldham (1980) identify five characteristics that contribute to the motivating potential of a job.
- *Skill variety*. Does the job have a variety of activities which use the different skills and talents of the job holder?
- *Task identity*. Does the job require the completion of a whole task or unit of work?
- *Task significance*. Does the job have a significant impact on the life and work of other people?
- *Autonomy*. Does the job provide the job holder with freedom and discretion in the organisation of the work?
- *Task feedback*. Does the job holder receive direct and helpful feedback while working?

PERFORMANCE MANAGEMENT AND THE WORK TEAM

In the continuing search for improved performance and better employee relations, many organisations are opting for teams as the basis for arranging work and workers. In some cases, 'team' is just a different term for 'work group' or 'section' or 'department'; there is little if any change to the way that work activities are allocated and carried out, and the traditional supervisory structure and behaviour remain largely intact.

There will be a significant impact on performance management where there is a genuine attempt to change patterns of work, to establish a different type of relationship between team members and their team leader, and among members of the team. Even then, the team and its results remain the responsibility of someone in the management system—although that person's focus will need to shift from individual performance to team performance. Some argue that the teamwork trend sounds yet another death knell for performance planning and review. Others are confident it will survive (just as it has survived other rumours of its demise, most recently because of its alleged conflicts with quality management). Indeed, performance management techniques, appropriately selected and applied, are important contributors to the success of team-working. After all, as with individuals, the team and its members need to know what is expected of them, how well those expectations are being met and what will happen next.

Some organisations opt for team-working but then continue with individual-based performance appraisal systems. Others abandon individual-based performance management after moving to team-working. Team-building and team performance probably suffer in both situations. Organisations need to take a balanced approach: they should plan, manage and review the development of individual employees and their contributions to the work team, and they should plan, manage and review the performance of the team as a unit. In other words, a distinction between the individual's contribution to the team and the group's overall performance is a critical factor in the planning and management of team performance. This distinction is discussed in more detail in Chapter 9.

Again, like individual performance, team activities and targets need to be managed within a context of the organisation's overall strategies and goals. A performance planning and review process is a useful tool for clarifying and aligning individual, team and organisational goals. Figure 2.2 shows how UK-based Glaxo Wellcome views this process.

PERFORMANCE MANAGEMENT AND THE 'NEW' EMPLOYEE

Today's employees are often described as different from their predecessors: more educated, more likely to question than to accept managerial authority, more focused on their own career development than on the organisation's interests, more mobile, less loyal, and so on. Many managers see these characteristics in a negative light, and advance them as yet more reasons why performance planning and review won't work.

In fact, these characteristics make today's employees—especially the so-called *knowledge workers*—a more valuable, and certainly more costly, organisational resource than the traditional white-collar and blue-collar workers. The jobs of these 'new' employees present new challenges for managers but, handled effectively, these challenges are a key to better

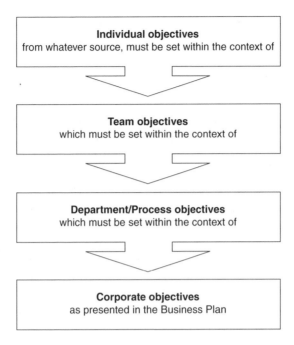

FIGURE 2.2   TEAM-WORKING AND OBJECTIVES SETTING

individual and organisational performance. For example, knowledge-based jobs might involve high levels of non-repetitive work, with frequent changes in demand and direction making prediction and planning much more difficult and uncertain.

Other features of knowledge work also have an impact on the management of performance.

- Knowledge workers often have the authority to decide their work priorities and their approaches to their work. Few managers, for example, would risk telling a highly qualified scientist how to undertake a particular research project.
- It may be difficult to quantify the outcomes of knowledge work. For example, 'number of completed transactions' might be an appropriate performance measure for a bank teller, but the 'number of lines of code written' by a computer programmer could well be a meaningless measure. The ability to solve problems is often the real key to effective performance of knowledge work.
- Knowledge workers usually work in situations where their 'output rates' are influenced by factors that they might not be able to control,

and where their work affects many other people inside and outside the organisation. This is very different from the machine operator whose work flows along the line at a predetermined speed.

- Knowledge workers seldom operate by themselves, but need to interact with others to achieve their goals.

These job characteristics are often reflected in the knowledge workers themselves. On the whole, they are well educated, adept at solving problems and high in self-motivation and self-esteem. They like being free to choose their work methods and will usually adapt quickly to working in groups. However, some of these features present special challenges when it comes to managing their performance.

The major issue may be the question of accountability. Many hospital doctors, for example, believe that their primary responsibility is to their patients, and they will resist and resent attempts by hospital authorities to manage them or their work. They claim that their loyalty to a professional ethos overrides any considerations of organisational planning and resource allocation. In this situation, counting the 'number of patients treated' might be important to a hospital which has to assess how well it controls its waiting lists, but the same measure might be anathema to the doctors whose principal concern is excellence in patient care. Doctors might also resent or reject being managed by people who are not their professional peers, even though those managers are superior to them in the organisational hierarchy. Other professionals—engineers and architects are good examples—might be more accustomed to working in organisations where professional desires and commercial considerations must be balanced, and where managing people and projects is part of normal processes and behaviour.

Such clashes of ethos can loom large. Usually, they mean that a performance planning and review system that would suit production workers or managers in a commercial enterprise will probably not be effective where there are large numbers of professional employees—and attempting to force such a system on these workers will probably be counterproductive.

Different approaches to performance review need to be found. Peer assessments are common among professional groups, especially for decisions about appointments or promotions, and these techniques can be adapted for more general performance review purposes. Tertiary education institutions now commonly ask students to evaluate the performance of their lecturers, although there have to be doubts about the relevance of some of the questions asked and concern at how much use is made of the information. One university professor told me that good lecturers are constantly looking for feedback on their performance and welcome suggestions for improvement; others hide their poor performance behind the cloak of academic freedom and independence.

There is no reason why professional groups within an organisation should not be subject to some form of performance management—even though a performance planning and review system for professional and knowledge workers should recognise very clearly that both the organisation and the employees have distinct needs which are not always in harmony. But that can be recognised and overcome by having those employees closely involved in discussing the need for performance management, how it might be developed and introduced, and what might be the outcomes. One outcome might be a better understanding of those distinct needs, and a coming together of the different groups. However unreasonable their initial attitudes and responses might seem, we need to remember that professional and other knowledge workers are, by definition, relatively highly educated; one of the things they have learned is how to question.

The differences between *traditional* and *new* employees have other implications for the transition from traditional performance appraisal techniques to a more holistic approach to performance management.

- **Loyalty and commitment**. It's often said that 'new' employees are less loyal and committed to their organisations than 'traditional' employees. Knowledge workers, for example, are said to be more committed to their own careers and more willing to switch employers in search of development opportunities. Traditional employees, on the other hand, are more concerned with job security.
- **Rewards**. All employees value remuneration, but new employees are likely to expect it to result more from their good performance than from long service or other factors.
- **Communication and participation**. New employees may be more interested in participation than traditional employees. Indeed, they may insist on being involved in decisions that affect them and their work. They expect to have more information about the organisation and its operations, and about their jobs.
- **Goals**. Traditional employees may focus more readily on long-term goals, such as a secure retirement, than new employees who have grown up in a world of change and mobility, and are thus less willing to postpone satisfaction and rewards.
- **Work**. New employees are seeking challenging and interesting work that offers opportunities to be creative and innovative. They are concerned with the value of their jobs to the organisation, and

possibly to the community as well. Traditional employees will accept routine jobs, and see interesting work as an unexpected bonus.

- **Work, family and leisure.** Traditional employees are content to put their jobs ahead of family and leisure; 'new' employees look for more balance between life and work.

Of course, the challenges brought by these changes go beyond performance planning and review. They affect the organisation's overall approach to people and performance management and development. However, a carefully designed system of performance management—one that is appropriate to the needs of both the people and the organisation—can be a powerful vehicle for establishing the improved communication and understanding that will be a key to future organisational success.

PANACEA OR DISEASE?

It would be wrong to see a performance management system—or, more particularly, a system of performance planning and review—as a cure for all management and organisational ills. But it is neither accurate nor helpful to dismiss performance appraisal, as Deming did, as a 'deadly disease'. Deming and his disciples in the quality movement criticised performance appraisal or evaluation on the grounds that it attributes variations in performance to individual employees and disregards the fact that employees work within groups and systems that they do not control. They argue that there is not much difference between the performance of individuals, that any differences are outside the individual's control and that, in any case, managers are unable to identify whether performance variations are derived from systems or individuals. As a consequence, performance appraisal systems encourage people to set 'safe' goals and to squeeze systems for individual gain rather than improve them for collective benefit.

There is no point in denying these criticisms, but they should be countered. We see in Chapters 4 and 5 that managers do find it difficult to assess the performance of employees accurately and consistently. However, systems that compare planned performance with actual performance help to lessen those difficulties and allow managers and employees to discuss problems with processes or relationships. Where systems drive behaviour—as on the traditional production line—it might be fair to say that differences between the performance of individuals will be marginal. It would be much more difficult to build such a case in the more frequent situations where employees do have significant control over the pace and quality of their work. Building that case would require us also to reject much of the research on human behaviour. If performance appraisals are seen as instruments of control and of management by 'fear', people will respond accordingly. This book prefers to see performance planning and review as an open approach to managing people and their performance.

CHAPTER 3

DEVELOPING A PERFORMANCE MANAGEMENT SYSTEM

Performance appraisal systems are often unpopular and unsuccessful because they are seen as just another add-on human resources management technique. In particular, people dislike the appraisal interview which, in many organisations, has to be done when managers are busy with plans, budgets and other year-end activities. A performance management approach, on the other hand, emphasises the year-round cycle of planning, monitoring, reviewing, rewarding and developing—and emphasises the benefits for both employees and the organisation.

After an extensive literature review, Bevan and Thompson (1991) concluded that a textbook performance management system would include these features.

* The organisation has a shared vision—a mission or values statement—which it communicates to all employees.
* Individual performance targets relate to both operating unit targets and wider organisational objectives.
* There are regular, formal reviews of progress towards performance targets.
* The review process is used to identify training, development and reward outcomes.
* The organisation evaluates the effectiveness of the performance management process so that changes and improvements can be made.

These findings are reflected in current organisational practice. A survey of Australian and New Zealand organisations taken in 2000, covering both the private and public sectors, found a number of performance management system characteristics which distinguished higher-performing organisations from those that were less successful (CCH 2000).

* Higher-performing organisations were more likely to link rewards for senior and middle-level managers and professionals directly to their performance appraisal and management system.

- Their performance management systems were more tightly integrated with their corporate and business-level strategies and plans, and with other human resources systems.
- Their performance management systems were used more extensively to communicate organisational strategies to employees.
- Both the procedural and distributive justice of their performance management systems were rated more highly.
- Their performance management systems were linked more explicitly to organisational consequences (e.g. rewards, development, promotions, exit).
- Action plans and follow-up were used more extensively after performance reviews.
- Their performance management systems had received greater attention and development in recent years.
- Formal reviews showed that the performance management systems of higher-performing organisations were more effective than those of lower performers.

Simply put, the performance management concept recognises that a sure way to improve the organisation's performance is to help its people improve their performance. To do this, we must communicate the organisation's objectives better, train and develop individual employees so that they can achieve agreed targets and objectives, and continually work to build better relationships between managers and employees.

Many appraisal systems—especially those rooted in the Management by Objectives or MBO tradition—focus strongly on the tasks to be done and the measures to be used to decide whether an individual's performance is satisfactory. This is the *process* approach. Behind it lies a belief that high performance is best achieved by first analysing what work must be done to achieve the required results and then designing the most efficient way for that work to be organised and carried out. Work study, organisation and methods, total quality management and payments by results make up some of the infrastructure used to support this approach—which assumes that employees will do things in the 'one best way' because it is in their interests to do so.

But the process approach does not encourage employees to see and understand how their work contributes to the overall performance and success of the organisation. A *people* approach, on the other hand, assumes that high performance can only be achieved through people. As Alan Fowler (1990) says:

> if the right people are selected for the right jobs in the right numbers, if they are trained in the appropriate skills, and if they are effectively

led and motivated, then they will inevitably work well. There is an assumption that, by and large, competent, motivated people will evolve their own best methods of working.

Of course, no organisation will have a purely *process* or purely *people* approach to performance management. People-based approaches need support from organisational systems, just as process-based approaches must recognise that the inputs of managers and other employees are important.

So the question is not whether you will have a process-based system or a people-based system: the challenge is to develop an approach to performance management that recognises the particular needs of the organisation and its people and fits with its style and culture and working methods. Far too often, new management techniques are introduced—usually imposed from the centre or the top—without much thought to their impact on style and culture. Not only is the new technique often incompatible—for example, when a highly structured appraisal system is brought into a relatively flexible and informal work environment—but it can also fail because no one is willing to accept *ownership* and, therefore, the responsibility to make it work.

DECIDING ON OBJECTIVES

In a famous article, Douglas McGregor (1957) wrote that formal performance appraisal systems are designed to meet three needs, one for the organisation and two for the individual.

- They relate to the development of employees by providing a basis for the coaching and counselling of staff by their managers.
- They are a means of telling employees how they are doing, of suggest-ing needed changes in behaviour, attitudes, skills or job knowledge, and of letting them know where they stand with the boss.
- They provide systematic judgments to back up salary increases, promotions, transfers and, sometimes, demotions or terminations.

Unfortunately, many appraisal systems grow over time into unwieldy and bureaucratic mechanisms which struggle along with multiple purposes and often conflicting goals. In other words, they try to do too much—and end up doing none of these things very well. Deciding what you want your system to do is an essential first step. Basically, there are two possibilities.

- **Performance planning and review.** *Performance plans* set out the agreed goals and targets for a particular period or project, and *performance reviews* assess progress towards achieving them. Reviews can also be used to assess an individual's behaviour, especially as a member of a work group or team.

The plan focuses on future behaviour and performance: What is the employee expected to do? How is the employee expected to behave or perform? What changes in behaviour or performance are desirable or required? The focus of the review is past performance: How well did the employee perform in terms of the agreed targets? How well did the employee contribute to the discussions and decisions of the team? The results of the review might then be used in deciding whether an employee is to receive a pay increase, or be promoted or transferred, or given more training, or terminated.

- **Personal and performance development.** There are three aspects to development. One is the planning of future performance, often with work targets being agreed between manager and employee. A second aspect relates to the employee's own development: what additional skills, knowledge or experience would enable the employee to make a better contribution? This is a basis for training plans, career development, promotion and transfer decisions, and so on. The third aspect is the development of a stronger and more open relationship between managers and their employees. This is accompanied by a desire, through recognition and support, to provide employees with greater motivation and to encourage them to greater commitment to the organisation and its values and goals.

Managing and developing individuals' performance and potential might be the main purposes for planning and review systems. But they have a third role as well. Organisations use formal performance planning and review as a control system to hold managers accountable for the behaviour and effectiveness of their employees. Managers, similarly, can use the system as a form of control over employees.

It is easy to see that managers and employees might become confused if the objectives and purpose of performance planning and review are not clear, and not reflected in the approach that everyone in the organisation takes and the behaviours they use.

Traditionally, performance appraisal emphasised appraisal. Today, many organisations would claim that they are more open in their performance planning and review methods and more development-oriented in focus. But is it seen like that in practice by employees, or managers? Or do employees go into a performance review expecting to be told what they did wrong or where their performance was inadequate, to set targets for increasing their work output—and then to be told their new salary and asked, incidentally, if there are any training courses they would like to attend? For many employees, the experience is a negative one, no matter how hard the manager tries to involve them in the discussion and seek their ideas and commitment.

What do organisations do?

Organisations have a wide range of objectives and purposes for their performance planning and review systems. The table shows the results of a survey of more than 500 Australian and New Zealand organisations (CCH 2000).

Performance planning and review objective	*Organisations with this objective (%)*
Identify training needs	92
Provide employees with self-development information	86
Set work objectives	72
Determine bonus and merit payments	66
Career planning	62
Workforce and succession planning	47
Decide on promotions	42
Review and update job descriptions	39
Legal purposes	37
Decide on transfers	17
Validate human resources practices (e.g. selection and training effectiveness)	16
Communicate organisation objectives and values	10

CONFLICTS

Part of the difficulty for both managers and employees is the almost inevitable conflict between the different roles and purposes in the performance planning and review process. Not all these conflicts can be resolved or removed but it helps to know about them.

The first conflict arises from the fact that the organisation and its employees have different goals: employees are seeking reassurance, reinforcement and, they hope, additional rewards, while the organisation wants them to accept constructive criticism in order to improve their performance and fulfil their potential. But is it likely that people will be open and frank about their skills weaknesses and performance lapses if they think this will jeopardise their chances of a promotion or pay increase? Similarly, few of us find it easy to be totally open and honest unless we have a strong and friendly relationship with our manager.

A second major source of conflict is the different roles that managers are expected to play—depending on the purpose of the performance review—as both *judge* and *helper*. Most managers find it difficult to play both these roles credibly at the same time. This strengthens the argument that performance management systems should be restricted to perform-ance-related matters and not extended to remuneration, training, career development and other areas of human resources management. Some organisations overcome this problem by having separate systems for *performance review* and *personal development*, or by holding separate performance and development interviews at different times.

These conflicts are summarised in Figure 3.1 and relate to the possible objectives of the process. When the objective is performance-related, the system can be a mechanism for managers to make difficult decisions that can affect both the long-term (e.g. promotion) and short-term (e.g. remu-neration) future of the employee. In communicating those decisions,

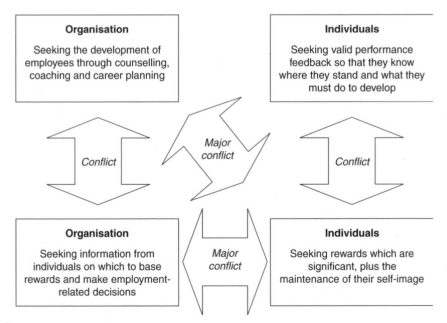

FIGURE 3.1   INEVITABLE CONFLICTS IN PERFORMANCE PLANNING AND REVIEW

What do you think?

Sooner or later every organisation has to make decisions about the performance management system it wants, and what the objectives are going to be. Unfortunately, this is an area where it's possible to agree with just about everyone—which leads to confusion. Here are a few questions to help you develop your thinking on some of the key issues. There are no right or wrong answers, and you might want to come back and review your responses as you read on.

1. Performance reviews should be concerned only with the personal development of the employee.

   Strongly   *Strongly*
   agree   *Agree*   *Not sure*   *Disagree*   *disagree*

2. Pay and promotion decisions should be based on performance review results.

   Strongly   *Strongly*
   agree   *Agree*   *Not sure*   *Disagree*   *disagree*

3. In my experience, pay and promotion decisions are based on performance review results.

   Strongly   *Strongly*
   agree   *Agree*   *Not sure*   *Disagree*   *disagree*

4. Performance reviews provide employees with accurate feedback.

   Strongly   *Strongly*
   agree   *Agree*   *Not sure*   *Disagree*   *disagree*

5. In my experience, managers and employees agree on performance plans and on the criteria for determining whether performance is good or not.

   Strongly   *Strongly*
   agree   *Agree*   *Not sure*   *Disagree*   *disagree*

6. Performance planning and review makes a difference. It motivates employees, leads to better performance, and increases understanding of employees' roles and managers' expectations.

   Strongly   *Strongly*
   agree   *Agree*   *Not sure*   *Disagree*   *disagree*

7. Managers and employees do performance planning and review only because the organisation requires it.

Strongly
agree   *Agree*   *Not sure*   *Disagree*   *Strongly*
disagree

8. Performance reviews should be based solely on goals and targets agreed earlier by the employee and the manager.

Strongly
agree   *Agree*   *Not sure*   *Disagree*   *Strongly*
disagree

9. Employees should review their own performance and this should be an important part of the total performance review.

Strongly
agree   *Agree*   *Not sure*   *Disagree*   *Strongly*
disagree

10. My experience with performance planning and review has been helpful in guiding my personal and professional development.

Strongly
agree   *Agree*   *Not sure*   *Disagree*   *Strongly*
disagree

11. Performance reviews usually leave me more uncertain about where I stand than I was before the discussion.

Strongly
agree   *Agree*   *Not sure*   *Disagree*   *Strongly*
disagree

12. The performance planning and review system in our organisation allows managers to communicate clearly to employees exactly where the managers stand.

Strongly
agree   *Agree*   *Not sure*   *Disagree*   *Strongly*
disagree

13. Performance review reports are consulted when top management is making decisions about pay increases, training and development opportunities, promotions and appointments.

Strongly
agree   *Agree*   *Not sure*   *Disagree*   *Strongly*
disagree

Adapted from Sashkin (1981)

managers must be prepared to justify them in the face of an employee's disagreement or displeasure. That discussion alone can cast the two people as adversaries, lower their mutual trust and compromise their ability to cooperate. Spoiling that relationship will, in turn, have an adverse effect on the developmental objectives of performance planning and review. The manager's role as coach and helper—drawing employees out, listening to their problems, getting them to develop their own solutions—involves rather different communication processes and skills than the task of communicating a set of appraisal decisions.

On the right-hand side of Figure 3.1, we can see employees' conflicting goals. Employees are looking for feedback because it helps to answer the questions 'How well am I doing?' and 'What do you think of my performance?' Positive feedback helps employees satisfy their psychological needs to feel appreciated and wanted. Critical feedback, by contrast, indicates some kind of failure and might be difficult for employees to accept. In other words, when people seek feedback they are usually seeking favourable comments that will reinforce their positive self-image. When rewards—pay and promotion, for example—are linked to performance reviews, employees will be even more reluctant to accept unfavourable feedback. When it comes to self-development, employees must be willing to accept feedback and suggestions from their managers.

The major source of conflict might be the simple fact that the organisation is not sure about the purpose of its performance planning and review system, and this lack of clarity continues through the ranks of the managers and their employees. For example, it will be difficult to persuade employees that management takes the system seriously when they discover that their own managers have not yet had performance planning and review discussions with their managers. Nor will they readily accept that the review discussion contributes to remuneration decisions when they are told, at the end of the interview, what management has decided their new remuneration will be.

Another conflict arises from the simple fact that, apart from the person at the very top and those at the very bottom of the organisational hierarchy, everyone in the organisation has roles as both 'reviewer' and 'reviewee'. If a manager's own experience of performance planning and review is not positive, that will probably carry through into the manager's performance planning and review with the next level of employees.

In addition, where there is a second-level or 'one-up' review, managers know there are two audiences for their assessments—the employee concerned and their own manager who has to review the review. The manager may have to sell the assessment twice—once upwards and once downwards—and that could be a temptation to play it safe. Moreover, managers appear to believe that employees regard specific suggestions for performance improvement as the most important aspect of their reviews, while their managers are looking mainly to justify their ratings or to see how they compare with the ratings given to other employees (McGuire 1980). The contradictions in these different perceptions are obvious.

At the very least, there is a problem of different perceptions. Many years ago, researchers studied the performance appraisal system at the General Electric Company, a system then regarded as 'state of the art'. Some of the results were a major surprise (Meyer et al. 1965).

- While 92 per cent of managers and 85 per cent of employees agreed that remuneration and promotion decisions should be based on performance reviews, only 68 per cent of managers and 49 per cent of employees thought this actually happened.
- Only 72 per cent of managers and 55 per cent of employees agreed that performance reviews provided accurate feedback based on a shared understanding of what was good or poor performance.
- Only 74 per cent of managers and 62 per cent of employees thought that performance appraisal made a difference.
- A staggering 57 per cent of managers and 63 per cent of employees agreed that performance reviews were carried out only because it was an organisational requirement.

We're left to wonder how different the responses might be today.

EFFECTIVE PERFORMANCE MANAGEMENT SYSTEMS

There is no best way to design and introduce a performance planning and review system. What works in one organisation might fail miserably in another. However, the experience of a wide range of organisations suggests that effective performance management systems share certain characteristics (Strebler et al. 2001).

- The performance management system has clear aims and measurable success criteria.
- Employees are involved in the design and implementation of the system.
- The system is simple to understand and operate.
- Effective use of the performance management system is at the core of managers' performance goals.
- The system allows employees a clear 'line of sight' between their performance goals and those of the organisation.

- The system focuses on role clarity and performance improvement.
- The focus on performance improvement is closely linked to an adequately resourced training and development infrastructure.
- The purpose of any direct link between the performance management system and employee rewards is made crystal clear, and proper equity and transparency safeguards are built in.
- The performance management system is regularly and openly reviewed against its own success criteria.

These findings can be developed into a series of guidelines for effective performance planning and review systems.

Get the objectives clear

An organisation must have a clear purpose for its performance planning and review system. Ideally, the focus should be tightly on performance. This can include *what* performance is expected and achieved as well as *how* employees carry out their job responsibilities and relate to others in the workplace. To keep the focus on performance, some organisations separate performance *planning and review* from performance or personal *development*. They recognise there is a conflict in objectives and style between appraisal and development discussions and, while accepting the obvious link between performance and development, make them the subject of separate manager–employee discussions. They often hold these discussions at different times of the year.

These organisations understand that there is likely to be more open and honest discussion—with less opportunity for defensive or self-justifying behaviour—when the manager's roles as *judge* and *helper* are split. At the same time, there are separate forms or records for the planning and review and development discussions so that the two objectives are not confused in the organisation's human resources information system either.

Set the right style

As well as getting the objectives clear, an organisation must set the right style for its performance management system. If the organisation is hierarchical and employees are not accustomed to being asked for their ideas and opinions, they're not very likely to be quick to make performance-related suggestions. In these situations, shared goal-setting is difficult: managers will believe that goals have been agreed with employees, but the employees are likely to feel that they've been assigned their work targets. Performance planning and review is as much a matter of style as system, and it may take a little time for people to adjust their behaviour and attitudes. Performance planning and review is a process, not an event.

Traditionally, we have considered it appropriate—mainly to encourage consistent communication and treatment—to have a single performance appraisal system throughout the organisation. Given the diversity of people and activities in the modern organisation, a single performance planning and review system might no longer be effective.

In other words, 'one size won't fit all'. For some employees, it will be appropriate to plan improvements or changes to performance and to set quantitative targets. For others, it will be more appropriate to decide on qualitative assessments of performance improvements or changes. Still other employees will be expected or required simply to bring their performance or output up to a particular level or standard, and then maintain it. And some types of workers will be assessed for their competencies—that is, for their capability to perform rather than for their actual performance. The members of specific work groups might be assessed for their team membership styles and contributions as well as, or instead of, being assessed for their individual performance or the group's results. Older employees might not see much point in discussing longer-term career development needs, but this will be important for younger staff. Similarly, the performance planning and review focus for a new recruit should be different from that for someone who has been in the job for a long time.

And we need to think carefully whether managers' performance targets should be related to their unit's output or to their own inputs to the systems, processes and relationships of the unit. This is not an argument for different performance planning and review systems for management and non-management employees. Differences in system and approach should be based on job content and work requirements, and on employees' skills and roles and experience, not on their level in the organisational hierarchy.

We should also recognise that some employees are more comfortable talking about themselves, their jobs and their performance than others. Sometimes this will be a function of people's communication skills or self-confidence. In other cases, it will reflect people's perceptions of their role and status in the organisation, or the power relationship between managers and employees. Employees who are seeking promotion or other forms of career development may want more feedback about their performance and potential than those who are reasonably satisfied with their present positions.

Thus, as far as possible, performance planning and review systems should probably let managers suggest what approach will be appropriate to use with different types of employees—and the employees themselves might be consulted on this question as well. In the end, an organisation will want to have the most effective performance planning and review system possible; using a single system across the whole organisation might weaken its usefulness and acceptability quite significantly.

However, in allowing flexibility, we should remember that some managers will continue to look for prescriptive rules for performance planning and review and will be uncomfortable if there aren't any. At the same time, others will be concerned at the possibility of inconsistent approaches and practices in different parts of the organisation, and a few might go outside the broad guidelines—often with good intentions—and then have to be brought back within them.

Reviews are part of a process

Performance reviews are only part of the process of performance management. You can reinforce this message by changing the name from *performance appraisal*, with its implications of judgment, to *performance planning and review*, which makes it clear that the process has two parts. It also signals that performance standards and targets will be set in advance, so that actual performance will be reviewed in terms of agreed goals.

However, we need to go further than this and establish that performance plans and reviews are just part of a continuing process of *performance management* which also involves managing, developing and rewarding performance. All the elements of the cycle need to be in place and given appropriate emphasis. In particular, we must recognise that the quality and usefulness of a performance planning and review discussion is greatly influenced by the strength of the relationships between managers and their employees. Managers should be providing feedback, advice and assistance on a continuing basis, so that the end-of-year interview is basically a summary of issues that have already been discussed. Performance planning and review discussions cannot by themselves produce open, trusting and mutually dependent relationships between managers and employees; the process does, however, work in the opposite direction.

Ask people to think about performance appraisals which they have found effective and worthwhile. Don't be surprised if they mention a positive relationship with the manager as a key influence. When the relationship between manager and employees is strong, there will be frequent two-way communication, a sharing of ideas and problems, and mutual feedback. In this way, performance planning and review becomes a useful technique for managing all year, not just on one day.

Think about timing

Many organisations expect managers to carry out all their performance reviews over a short time period, often at the end of the year when managers are busy finalising the previous period's reports and accounts and trying to prepare next year's plans and budgets. It should be no great surprise that managers often see performance appraisals as another irritation, imposed upon them by a corporate office or human resources department which doesn't understand the pressures under which they work.

To overcome this problem, some organisations spread performance planning and review discussions throughout the year—scheduling sessions, for example, on the anniversary of the employee's appointment to the organisation or the job. In most cases, this will spread the workload more evenly, giving the manager time to prepare, avoiding end-of-year pressures and making performance discussions a normal part of being a manager. As long as the system allows for interim discussions of both targets and achievements, there is no reason why individual employees should feel that these performance plans and reviews are detached from the organisation's planning cycle.

You should also think about the frequency of performance discussions. An annual cycle might not be appropriate for people whose work is project-based: they should probably plan and review their performance at each stage of the project. New employees probably need to start with more frequent performance discussions, setting plans and reviewing performance at intervals of, say, three months during the first year.

Ironically, just when managers are coming to understand the need to give employees more opportunities and responsibility for making their own work decisions, an increasingly turbulent environment suggests there is a growing need for more frequent performance discussions. Again, we need to separate day-to-day interactions from the wider, more strategic discussion, and ensure that the purpose and style of performance planning and review are not closer supervision or scrutiny of employees' work, but a more systematic overview of the key aspects of their performance.

We should also remember that changes which affect performance plans are happening all the time. Targets should change too. Employees may become aggrieved and lose trust in a process that reviews their performance against targets which they now consider irrelevant and unrealistic. To guard against this, some organisations ask managers to meet with employees every three months for interim reviews of their performance plans. This need not be a full-scale performance discussion: a quick check on progress and adjustment to directions or targets will usually be enough.

Keep remuneration decisions separate

Performance pay has become a central feature of remuneration systems in recent years, although there is much doubt about the linkage between pay and performance and considerable debate about the effectiveness of pay-for-performance rewards systems.

We have seen already how openness and disclosure in the performance discussion could be adversely affected if employees think there might be negative consequences for decisions about their rewards. It is one of performance appraisal's inherent conflicts. Two other points should be made. First, if employees lack confidence in the appraisal system, why should they accept the remuneration decisions it produces? Second, despite the popularity of performance pay, the fact is that organisations pay people for more than their performance. Moreover, if people see a direct link between performance and pay, what is the likelihood they will then focus on those activities that promise increased remuneration, possibly to the detriment of their other job responsibilities?

Despite these problems, employees seem to feel that rewards should be discussed during the formal performance review. It gives a serious focus to an employee's performance targets and achievements and answers the question 'How will I be rewarded for my contribution?' The answer, however, need not be in specific dollar terms at the time of the discussion. The performance–pay debate is continued in Chapter 8.

Forms don't matter

Unfortunately, we seem to be better at designing appraisal forms than at developing and implementing effective performance management systems— or at managing performance well. We must get better at the things that matter, which means shifting the emphasis from form-filling to planning, monitoring and reviewing performance. Forms are simply a means of recording what has been discussed and agreed; too often, completing the forms becomes the main purpose of the performance discussion.

However, it is important for performance plans and reviews to be recorded accurately and for those records to be kept with appropriate confidentiality and security. Increasingly, employees have legal rights to challenge management's decisions—on both procedural and substantive grounds—and the organisation might have to produce the performance planning and review documents which contain the information they relied on in making the decisions in question. As we see in Chapter 5, requirements for fairness and equity will also influence the organisation's choice of a performance planning and review approach.

Focus on performance not personality

Personality traits often feature on appraisal forms, with job performance included as a secondary factor. This emphasis is wrong. No one has yet defined with confidence the ideal personality profile for any particular position. And what is the precise meaning of terms such as 'integrity' or 'reliability'? How do you differentiate between 'self-confident' and 'aggressive'?

There is less likelihood of unconscious discrimination in performance reviews which concentrate on performance. Many personality-related descriptors are heavily value-laden, and the lack of objective criteria for assessing such characteristics opens the way for bias. This becomes particularly important when information from performance reviews is used for decisions about pay or promotion, or for selecting people for training and development programs. If the criteria and the assessment are not demonstrably objective, the employer may be open to allegations of discrimination.

In the United States, courts have held as invalid such subjective criteria as 'adaptability', 'maturity' and 'drive', because they allow for conscious or unconscious prejudice. They have also decided that assessments based on 'leadership ability', 'experience', 'cooperation' and 'dependability' are subjective and open to bias (Townley 1990).

But there is a much more compelling reason for concentrating on performance. The simple fact is that managers can do little or nothing about an employee's personality—but they can influence performance in various ways. In other words, managers will be more effective if they concentrate on the *what* and *how* of an employee's performance and leave *why* to the psychologists!

Encourage participation

Managers and employees should discuss and, preferably, agree their performance plans and reviews, yet many people find this difficult. Why? One reason might be the traditional focus on *personality* discussed in the previous paragraph. People can feel awkward when asked to talk about themselves, especially if the discussion is about traits such as 'leadership' and 'friendliness'. Discussion easily descends into resentful arguments or sullen silence. Talking about previously agreed targets is likely to be more constructive and less emotionally charged.

Second, the traditional emphasis on a once-a-year discussion obscures the fact that reviewing progress and setting short-term goals should be routine for both managers and employees. None of us is very good at, or comfortable with, anything we do only once a year—another reason why an annual performance discussion might be a rather stilted and nervous experience. Managers and employees both need practice if their performance planning and review sessions are to be truly open and participative. At the same time, performance discussions can become artificial and self-conscious if the approach is too mechanical. Detailed forms and carefully rehearsed interviews are no substitute for openness, sincerity, naturalness and a genuine desire to help improve performance.

Increasingly, employees are being encouraged to prepare for the performance discussion, by reviewing their actual performance against the agreed plans and targets, and by thinking about future plans and targets. This preparation certainly reduces the chances that the communication will be all one-way. And, just as some employees actively seek feedback from their managers, managers can be encouraged to seek comments and suggestions on their own performance from the people who experience it most directly. With *upward appraisal*, employees are asked to provide, not just receive, feedback. Employees are specifically asked how they are managed, and whether the content and style of management is helpful to them in carrying out their job responsibilities. Handled sensitively in the right atmosphere, upward appraisal can help to open up the dialogue between managers and employees and break down the authoritarian nature of their traditional power relationship.

In another development, performance reviews are being based on information gathered from people all around the subject employee: *360-degree appraisal*, or *multi-rater review systems*, are discussed in Chapter 5.

Keep performance planning and review in management hands

Performance planning and review is not an optional extra for managers. They must help their staff to set and achieve work targets in line with the organisation's plans and they must review results with them. Performance planning and review is a tool of management accountability and employee motivation, although it should probably stress the manager's role as helper rather than judge. Specialists can play a role in developing and implementing performance management systems, but the systems should be run by line managers if they are going to make a continuing contribution and not be seen as an exercise in filling out forms for the human resources department.

In addition, performance planning and review should be kept in the hands of the appropriate level of management. Essentially, the process is part of the relationship between each manager and each employee, which means that managers should be held accountable for planning and reviewing the performance of those who report to them. Only in special cases will the views of higher managers, or managers elsewhere in the organisation, be important. The relationship between manager and employee is easily disrupted if the employee realises that the review comes from two or three levels up, if only to the extent that performance targets and results are then adjusted to reflect what is acceptable to higher management. Similarly, both managers and employees will be more cautious in their discussions (and the recording of them) if they know that the performance review form has to be sent to the human resources department for scrutiny.

Higher-level managers should ensure that performance plans and reviews are done, and done well, but should not interfere in the content of a review unless there is clear evidence of bias or some other problem. Those higher-level managers should—as part of planning and reviewing the performance of those who work for them—insist on better plans and reviews and work with their managers to achieve that goal. If the organisation needs information for planning or administrative purposes, that can be requested directly from managers. Frankly, the information in appraisal reports is often inadequate or unreliable for work-force planning, training and development or other purposes, and few human resources departments do much with the forms except file them.

Of course, the main reason for keeping performance planning and review in the hands of managers is to instil a sense of *ownership*. If managers are not involved in the development, implementation and ongoing maintenance of the system, they will be less committed to it. And without the commitment of managers throughout the organisation, no system of performance planning and review can work.

Unfortunately, as we noted at the start of this book, managers do not generally enjoy assessing performance and providing feedback to the people who work from them. Douglas McGregor (1957) pointed this out many years ago, observing that 'even managers who admit the necessity of (appraisal) programs frequently balk at the process—especially the interview part', mainly because they dislike being made to 'play God' over their subordinates. Other research has shown how managers can feel guilty about appraisals, regarding them as a hostile and aggressive act against employees.

Managers must be helped to overcome these feelings. This can best be done by encouraging them to accept performance management as their key role and responsibility, with performance planning and review the means for carrying out that role. Managers must be encouraged to see both the purpose and process of performance management in a positive light.

Insist on benefits

Performance discussions must produce results, for both managers and employees. They should not be seen negatively as tools of administration. They should be forward looking, not merely an audit of the past year. The employee should be an active participant, not just a passive object for analysis. These are easy propositions to state but, for most organisations, the reality is rather different.

Studies show that both managers and employees think the idea of performance review is good because it allows people to know where they stand. In practice, few managers initiate periodic discussions of performance with their employees unless they are required to do so. Managers claim to see the benefits of performance planning and review—but their behaviour often tells us something different. Those same studies show that few people can recall examples of constructive action taken or significant improvements achieved after a formal performance interview.

OVERCOMING OBJECTIONS

Anyone with experience of performance planning and review will have faced a wide range of objections and criticisms. They must be overcome if the organisation is to make an effective approach to this important aspect of the performance management process.

We've had appraisal systems before— they've never worked

Systems never work by themselves: people make systems work. However, people will only make systems work if they consider them useful and relevant, and if they have some commitment to them. Involving people in the design and implementation of the performance planning and review system will help to make it relevant and acceptable. Use the expertise of the human resources department and other specialists—but keep them in the background.

A first step in developing a new approach might be to ask both managers and employees why the old system didn't work. Grappling with the problems they identify, and overcoming them, could be the recipe for future success.

Top management isn't interested

If the organisation's top management doesn't actively support and partic-ipate in performance planning and review, it's not very realistic to expect other managers to be enthusiastic, or to expect employees generally to be serious about the system. In organisations with effective performance planning and review systems, the process begins with the chief executive and top managers and is 'owned' by all the managers. This means that those who want to develop or introduce performance planning and review might try to identify and encourage one or more top managers to champion or sponsor the idea. In the same way, systems that are devel-oped by managers themselves, rather than internal or external special-ists, have a better chance of working effectively even though they might not be ideal in design terms.

I don't know how the system works

Performance planning and review happens once a year in most organi-sations. As a result, managers and employees aren't constantly thinking about performance planning and review. Nor are they practising the skills and techniques used in performance discussions. To overcome this problem, the organisation needs to have adequate explanatory material about the performance planning and review system and how it works. This information may need to be revised and reissued before each round of performance discussions (if there is an annual cycle), supported perhaps by briefing sessions to remind both managers and employees how the system works.

Remember also that there will be new people in the organisation, or people who are new to the manager's role, since the last round of performance discussions. They might need more detailed information or assistance.

Some organisations hold special training courses on communication skills for use in performance planning and review sessions. Of course, face-to-face communication skills should be part of every manager's training and it might give a wrong emphasis to suggest that the skills needed to discuss performance are somehow separate or different. More worthwhile would be sessions for both managers and employees on how the system operates, how to formulate appropriate performance targets and develop relevant performance measures, and how to use the system's documentation. Communication in the discussion should be improved if both participants have had the same briefings and information.

There's never any follow-up or feedback

From their experience, many employees have little reason to expect that much will happen as a result of their performance reviews. It's not surprising, therefore, that people can be cynical about the process. An obvious and easy way to break down that cynicism is to make sure there *is* follow-up and feedback. Managers should ensure that employees are provided with the resources and support they need to achieve the agreed targets, and make time for regular progress checks with employees. When there is follow-up and feedback, employees will see the performance planning and review process as worthwhile and will be more willing to participate. That, in turn, will make the manager's job easier and more enjoyable.

It takes too much time

Unless it is an integral part of their roles and they recognise how it can work for them, busy managers might see performance planning and review as just another irritant imposed on them from above. Yet an investment of two or three hours a year in each of the organisation's 'most important assets' is hardly excessive when compared with the time absorbed by scheduled and unscheduled maintenance of plant and machinery.

Forms and documentation are another part of the time problem. Some performance appraisal forms run to twenty pages. It's almost inevitable that completing such documentation becomes a more important objective than discussing performance. Forms should be kept simple and used just as a way to record the discussion and agreement between two people.

My job can't be measured

Setting targets and objectives for different types of jobs is critical to performance planning and review. Distinctions can be drawn between *quantitative* and *qualitative* objectives and between performance *goals* and *standards*. Each organisation needs to think through these issues for itself, but remember what Einstein said: what cannot be measured cannot be done. Quality guru W. Edwards Deming went a step further, saying that things that cannot be measured probably should not be done.

They're more concerned with who I am than what I do

Systems based on personality traits and characteristics, or interviews and appraisals based on managers' judgments or opinions of employees are not very useful. The emphasis should be on observable job-related behaviours and their outcomes, and on descriptive feedback rather than judgments.

My job has changed: these priorities and targets are irrelevant

Many organisations build quarterly or six-monthly reviews into an annual planning and review cycle to allow for a rapidly changing environment. Nevertheless, there are many jobs where the activities, priorities and objectives remain quite similar over long periods. In some cases, the problem with irrelevant objectives is that they were initially set in too much detail or at too low a level.

Things are changing too fast for us to make plans

There's a cliché that people who fail to plan are planning to fail. No one denies that today's organisations operate in constantly and rapidly changing environments, in situations that are less predictable and more uncertain. But surely this increases the need for managers and their staff to clarify their roles and expectations on a regular basis? If they don't, chaos and confusion are likely—and apparently acceptable.

These are my boss's objectives, not mine

It's generally agreed that people commit more readily to objectives that they help to establish and agree with, but there will always be some aspects of a job where decisions have to be made without the direct involvement of the job holder. In such cases the performance planning and review process should help the employee understand and accept the reasons for the decision.

My staff are happy the way things are: they don't want this

How do you know? What do they say when you ask them? In fact, most employees say they would welcome an opportunity for a structured discussion about their current performance and their future goals and targets. But they too have been frustrated by cumbersome documentation, lack of management commitment, irrelevant job descriptions and unrealistic performance targets, artificial appraisal interviews, inadequate feedback, lack of follow-up—and all the other objections.

CHAPTER 4

PLANNING PERFORMANCE

Most appraisal systems put too little emphasis on planning performance—on setting out just what employees are expected to achieve in terms of quantity or quality or time frames, on checking that they have the necessary skills and knowledge, on ensuring that the organisation can make the necessary resources available, on determining what will happen if the expected levels and standards of performance are, or are not, met—and on gaining employees' agreement and commitment to all these decisions.

Without performance plans that are carefully and well made, there has to be a risk that the end-of-year interview will become a session for allocating fault and blame for what has not happened, rather than a no-surprises occasion for reviewing achievements, perhaps celebrating excellence, and planning future performance.

As we saw in Chapter 2, an employee's first questions are 'What do you want me to do?' and 'How well do you want me to do it?' The answers should be found in a job description or similar document.

PERFORMANCE PLANNING AND THE JOB DESCRIPTION

It is depressing how often employees reject their job descriptions as inaccurate, irrelevant or out of date. There are two major reasons for this: one is that the job description *is* inaccurate, irrelevant or out of date; the second is that the job description is often prepared for some purpose (commonly job evaluation, which few people in the workplace understand) or by a person who is remote from the immediate relationship of employee and manager.

The solution to this problem is to put the responsibility for job analysis, job design and job description in the hands of managers and employees. They might need and, indeed, welcome expert help from the human resources specialists. But the aim should be for the actors in this little drama to agree on a document that accurately sets out their roles and mutual expectations. The organisation may well need data about jobs for job evaluation, and for career path or organisation succession planning, and for many other worthwhile purposes. But the data needed for these purposes is quantitatively and qualitatively different from what we need for job descriptions for performance planning and review—that is, for managing people and their performance.

As you can see from the definitions set out in Figure 4.1, *job descriptions* and *person profiles* are two outcomes of the process of *job analysis*. *Job evaluation* is another outcome, but this activity is linked only tenuously to performance management.

Some people argue that job descriptions are neither necessary nor appropriate in today's fast-moving world. They claim, for example, that:

- Job descriptions are made obsolete by new organisational systems and structures, frequent changes in job roles and work requirements,

---

Job analysis

Job analysis involves gathering data about a specific job and what a person needs to do that job. It covers the job's objectives, functions, activities and relationships; the skills, knowledge and abilities needed by a job holder for effective performance; and the activities or targets that are used in assessing performance. In short, why does this job exist, what does it involve and where does it fit in the organisation?

Job description	**Person profile**	**Job evaluation**
A job description sets out in a logical form the work that is actually done and the reasons for doing it. It sets out the job's relationships inside and outside the organisation, and outlines what it is expected to contribute to the achievement of the organisation's overall goals. Its focus is the job, not the job holder.	This is a statement of the skills, knowledge and other attributes which are needed for effective performance in the job. It sets out any qualifications, experience or other job-related attributes which a person might reasonably be expected to have before being appointed to the position. It flows from the job description and is used to help match people to positions, and to identify training and development needs and priorities.	Job evaluation is used to measure the relative size or importance of jobs. It focuses on the content of the job itself, not on the job holder's actual or intended performance. It measures the job, not the job holder.

FIGURE 4.1   DEFINITIONS

the increasing use of team work and greater reliance on temporary and contingent workers.

- Job descriptions are accurate only so long as the present organisation of the work continues.
- Conventional job analysis and job descriptions can't cope with changes in the nature of work, such as reduced specialisation and greater sharing of work assignments (Morgan & Smith 1996).
- Job descriptions force organisations to draw boundaries, which are inconsistent with cross-training assignments, job and task rotation, self-managing teams and increasing devolution of responsibility (Carson & Stewart 1996).

These arguments have validity, of course. Yet, so long as the job—a collection of work tasks or activities assigned to an individual or, perhaps, a team—continues to be the basic unit of organisation and work design, then people will need job descriptions or similar documents as the essential road maps for their organisational journeys. But the criticisms are a reminder that job descriptions must be kept up to date, useful, fresh and relevant. That need not be a major challenge.

WRITING JOB DESCRIPTIONS

There are many ways of writing job descriptions. The form they take is not important so long as they set down clearly what the job holder is to do and the context in which those activities are to be performed. Some organisations have a standard format for job descriptions, although the risk here is that managers and employees will complete the form in order to satisfy what they see as an organisational requirement, and not because they regard the job description as helpful in their working relationship. In addition, if job descriptions are prepared to meet what is seen as a bureaucratic demand, or are routinely prepared by specialist job analysts or job description writers, the managers and employees directly affected by the job descriptions will feel no sense of ownership—and thus feel no great desire to ensure that the descriptions are kept accurate and up to date.

An organisation might have a set of generic or model job descriptions, but these should probably be used by managers and employees only as a basis for developing and agreeing their own description of the job the employee really does. In many instances, the interests, experiences, likes and dislikes of the individual job holder influence the actual content of the job, the priorities given its various aspects, and how the job is carried out. A generic job description cannot reflect those individual influences, but they should be recognised by both managers and employees in the performance planning and review process. One way to do this (see Figure 4.2) is to combine the job description and the performance plan.

These four broad guidelines for preparing effective job descriptions (Ungerson 1983) have stood the test of time.

Job descriptions should be simple

Many job descriptions are so complex that both managers and employees resist or ignore them. Lengthy statements of duties, authorities, responsibilities and accountabilities can cause confusion when, in fact, you seldom need all that detail. Job descriptions should concentrate on *actions* and *accountabilities*. They should be written clearly and simply, using the typical language of the workplace.

Job descriptions should not overstate or exaggerate

The key to a successful job description is accuracy. Jobs and their responsibilities are often exaggerated, either by including unimportant tasks and duties or by using inflated wording. Be careful that 'filing' does not become 'controls, issues and maintains inwards and outwards correspondence, plus other varied documentation'. Frequently, people know that the job description is to be used for job evaluation and exaggerate the job's responsibilities and importance in the hope of justifying a higher evaluation and, they hope, a higher salary.

Job descriptions should not be confused with person profiles

Job descriptions and person profiles are different and should be kept separate. Job descriptions containing a mixture of information about both the job and the ideal job holder are often confused and confusing. This has become a particular problem in organisations that have taken up the competency concept. Very often, their descriptions tell you more about the job holder's desirable qualities than the job's actual contents. You need both.

Job descriptions should be produced jointly and agreed

Job descriptions should not be written and imposed on job holders from above, nor be written by a job analyst working in isolation. Analysts might train managers to prepare descriptions, but the responsibility should remain with the managers and the job holders. After all, they will—or at least should—make most use of the job description. However the description is prepared, its contents should be agreed by both the job holder and the manager.

JOB DESCRIPTIONS AS PERFORMANCE CONTRACTS

Traditionally, the job descriptions found in many organisations have listed a range of tasks and duties. It is still not uncommon to find a list of ten or fifteen activities followed by the catch-all phrase 'such other duties as may be required from time to time'. Today, when the emphasis is on performance and achievement, it is more useful to set out the main objectives of the job and the related key results areas. In other words, a job description should not be a detailed list of day-to-day duties and activities: instead, it should describe those things for which the employee is to be held responsible or accountable. Grouping activities into results areas can help to simplify descriptions, avoid duplications and omissions, and sift out minor activities that are unimportant overall.

It is also possible (as shown in Figure 4.2) to use the job description to detail the expected performance standards and the measurement information relating to each key results area. A job description in this form addresses three key questions which employees have: What do you want me to do? How well do you want me to do it? How will I know when it's done?

The left-hand column of the job description (Figure 4.2) sets out the job's responsibilities in terms of expected results; the centre column establishes specific and measurable performance standards for each results area; and the right-hand column provides the controls or checks which enable the job holder and the manager to monitor progress and results.

In this way, the job description becomes a kind of *performance contract* between employee and manager (on behalf of the organisation). This gives the job description real significance, and it's an incentive for both the manager and the employee to ensure that the description is accurate, relevant and up to date—and that they are agreed on its contents. And, since it will be the framework for the next performance review, they will be encouraged to reconsider and revise the job description if there are any significant changes to the organisation's circumstances or the job's requirements. Indeed, 'renegotiation' of the job description should become a regular feature of their relationship, not in an adversarial way, but simply because it makes good sense for both parties to base their working relationship on an accurate and agreed document.

Job description

Position	Manager, Warehouse and Distribution
Department	Production
Date prepared	June 2003

Manager's signature ....

Job holder's signature ....

Position purpose

Provides leadership and guidance to warehouse and distribution team members to ensure that customers receive the products they order in good condition and on time.

Reports to	Production Manager

Responsible for	Warehouse assistants (4)	Van driver
	Administration Officer	

Functional relationships	Sales and Marketing Manager	Accounts Team Leader
	Sales executives	Human Resources Manager
	Team Leader, Final Assembly	Health and Safety Adviser

Authorities	**Financial**
	Approves expenditure within agreed operating budget
	Contracts
	Recommends courier and other transport contracts for approval of Production Manager
	Staffing
	Makes recommendations for approval of Production Manager

Key results areas	Performance standards	Reporting information
Warehouse and distribution staff have knowledge, skills, leadership and direction they need for satisfactory performance	Job descriptions, performance plans and reviews, and development plans are in place for all employees	Six-monthly activity report to Production Manager Performance plans and reviews are passed to Production Manager for information and review
	Employees are aware of workplace hazards and trained in safe working practices, handling hazardous materials, safe use of equipment and processes, and proper use of safety devices	Six-monthly report to Production Manager, with supporting audit by Health and Safety Adviser

FIGURE 4.2 SAMPLE JOB DESCRIPTION *(CONTINUES)*

Key results areas	Performance standards	Reporting information
Customer satisfaction is enhanced by accurate and on-time delivery of orders	Standard for local customers is same-day (preferably) or next-day delivery	Immediate report of stock shortages to Production Manager following comparison of sales orders and inventory control information
	For all other national deliveries, the standard is next-day delivery where overnight courier service is available, and a maximum of three days for all other orders	Immediate report of late deliveries to Sales and Marketing Manager and Production Manager
Warehouse housekeeping contributes to efficient operations and maintenance of pleasant and safe workplace; careful handling and storage ensure stock is clean and undamaged	Housekeeping and handling meet company requirements and standards	Monthly inspection by Production Manager and Health and Safety Adviser
	No orders rejected by customers because of appearance or damage	Immediate report of complaints or rejects to Sales and Marketing Manager and Production Manager
	No more than 1% of warehouse stock is returned to factory for rework because of dirt or damage	Three-monthly report to Production Manager on returns
Warehouse and distribution operating plans and budgets are prepared in line with company requirements and objectives and implemented following approval	Draft plans and budgets are prepared in the required format and time frame	
	Warehouse and distribution costs are kept within agreed budget levels	Monthly report of budget/actual expenditure to Production Manager
	Additional expenditure requires prior approval of Production Manager	

FIGURE 4.2   SAMPLE JOB DESCRIPTION

STANDARDS, TARGETS, OBJECTIVES AND MEASURES

Performance standards and work targets or objectives are central to most performance planning and review systems, which is a good reason for including them in the job description. It makes sense for employees to be able to find out about their key responsibilities and the expected performance standards in one place, but very little sense for these to be separated between the job description and the performance planning and review system.

Unfortunately, there is room here for confusion. A variety of terms are used to express performance plans—for example, goals, targets, objectives, measures, standards, indicators—and different people and organisations use these terms to mean different things. That's not important. What is important, to avoid confusion, is that the terms have the same meaning for all the people within a particular organisation.

One approach is to see work as purposeful activity in which we can distinguish between the purpose of the activity and the steps we take to achieve that purpose. The purpose of the organisation is often called its *vision* or *mission statement*, or it may be set out as a statement of *goals* or *aims*. These terms all mean much the same thing, and are typically stated broadly and with long time horizons.

The overall purpose can then be broken down into the things that have to be done to achieve it. These usually have a shorter and more defined time frame and contain some measurable elements. They may be called *targets* or *objectives*, and often relate specifically to the job holders in the organisation.

It can be helpful to see a target or objective as temporary: once it has been achieved the job holder moves on to another target or objective. Goals, aims and mission statements, by contrast, are longer lasting. They describe the reason for an organisation's existence and the direction in which it wants to go; targets and objectives set out the steps the organisation will take to reach its vision and achieve its long-term goals.

Key results areas

Terms like 'key results area' are commonly used to describe a critical area of a job's responsibilities from which significant results are required in a particular time period. For example, the manager and an employee might agree that Sales and Customer Relations are *key results areas* at the time of a new product launch. They will then agree on *targets* or *objectives* in the areas of Sales and Customer Relations.

Objectives and standards

An *objective* or *target* is a statement of the particular outcomes to be achieved in a key results area. When it is achieved, the job holder looks for a new target or objective. A *standard* describes performance criteria that are to be met on a continuing basis, usually by a fully trained and experienced employee. Thus, the performance standard for a particular machine might be 'the production of ten units each hour', whereas the performance target or objective for a trainee on that machine might be 'to produce five units each hour that meet the required quality levels'. In this way, *objectives* and *standards* both describe measurable performance expectations.

Performance indicators and measures

The terms 'performance indicator' and 'performance measure' are often used interchangeably to describe the evidence or information needed to show that a planned effort has achieved the desired results—in other words, that the target or objective has been met.

We can also use the terms to distinguish between performance *measures*—where the information needed is precisely measurable and unambiguous, usually in quantitative terms—and performance *indicators*, where it is not possible to obtain a precise measure. Performance indicators can also identify areas of activity where the organisation might compare its performance with other organisations. Kaufman (1988) suggests that performance measures and indicators can be used in two ways: in a *proactive* way to identify what should be done or accomplished, and *retrospectively* to provide criteria for determining success or failure. In addition, he suggests there are two types of measures or indicators. Some are *results-orientated*: they identify measurable performance and results, including individual contributions as well as organisational outcomes. Others are *implementation-orientated* and identify whether activities are in line with the organisation's goals and comply with its policies and procedures.

A further distinction can be drawn between *means* and *ends*. Probably the most useful measures or indicators are those that deal with *ends*—with results, outcomes, consequences and achievements. Those that focus on *means*, on how something is to be done and the facilities, methods and resources to be used, are useful mainly for providing feedback or to check progress towards the achievement of a planned target or desired result. They are also useful in situations where *how* an employee behaves is more important than *what* is actually achieved.

Performance measures and indicators can deal with both means and ends, but should distinguish between them. Depending on the level and type of job, goal-setting should be concerned mainly with results but those results need not be expressed only in terms of quantitative outputs. At the same time, the means to a particular end will not usually be included in the statement of the target or goal unless it is important to the achievement of that goal. In most situations, *what* employees do is more important than *how* they do it.

Whatever form they take, performance measures and indicators will be concerned with three key issues:

- **Economy**. Can we achieve the same results with fewer resources?
- **Efficiency**. Can we achieve more or better results with the same resources?
- **Effectiveness**. Have we achieved our goals and objectives?

PRINCIPLES AND BENEFITS OF PERFORMANCE MEASUREMENT

Before we can plan performance, we need to know how it will be measured. Jac Fitz-enz (1984) suggests some principles for performance measurement.

- *The productivity and effectiveness of any function can be measured by some combination of cost, time, quantity or quality indices.* Although some jobs are measured much more easily than others, all jobs can provide some indicators that are capable of measurement.
- *A measurement system promotes productivity by focusing attention on the important issues, tasks and objectives.* If employees are unsure about their work priorities, they will fill their time doing something, but being busy in this way might not meet an actual business need. Measurement helps people understand what to do, and why to do it.
- *Professional and knowledge workers are best measured as a group.* Professional and knowledge-based work calls for continuing learning and cooperation. Working as a team creates more favourable outcomes than individualistic activity which leads to competition within the group. Better results are achieved by measuring the performance of the whole group, based on clearly understood objectives. Members of a strongly cohesive group will do their own policing: they know who is contributing and who is not.
- *Managers can be measured by the efficiency and effectiveness of the units they manage.* The nature of a manager's work involves getting things done through other people. When assessing the quality of a manager's output, it is better to assess the success of the unit rather than the manager's personal work performance.
- *The ultimate measurement is effectiveness, not efficiency.* Effectiveness is concerned with getting results, doing the right things at the best time. It is a holistic concept in the sense that success should not

be narrowly assessed, but seen to flow from various aspects of the organisation's functioning.

But what are the benefits of performance measurement? Many critics quote Deming's description of performance appraisal as one of the seven deadly sins of management, a label he bestowed because of performance appraisal's alleged focus on measurable results to the exclusion of a more desirable concentration on organisational systems and processes. With respect, the great man missed the point. Performance targets and measures do not need to be constructed in quantitative terms, nor must they be concerned only with numerically measurable outcomes. Yet anything that is worthwhile to do must be capable of measurement in some way.

In other words, targets should be formulated in areas that have significance or importance for the organisation's goals and plans at a particular time. Those targets might be about increased production quantities; they might also, or instead, be about improving customer satisfaction, or achieving new standards of quality, or lifting employee morale, or whatever the organisation decides is important and relevant to its current goals.

Performance measurement has three main benefits.

- *People become focused on the critical success factors.* When there is an effective system of performance measurement, the focus of attention for employees is whatever is being measured and reported.
- *A measurement system helps to clarify goals and targets.* A measurement system is also a communication system. It tells employees what is expected of them. It clarifies the expected standards of performance and sets out what variations are acceptable. This enables employees to see, accept and understand the organisation's goals.
- *A measurement system provides employees with a challenge.* An effective measurement system can help staff to achieve and then exceed their performance targets. Each employee has the potential for a unique perspective on the work to be done, and how it might be done most effectively. Measurements that focus on outcomes and results can unlock employees' creativity, while people in strong and cohesive teams will enjoy the challenge of finding new and better ways to get the job done.

SETTING TARGETS

Just what motivates people to perform is hotly debated. It's a complex subject with a wide range of theories and techniques. Many of them are based on the idea that having a specific achievement in mind—a task, a quota, a standard, an objective or a deadline—plays an important part in motivating employees to perform. Having targets is itself an effective motivator of performance. It does not seem to matter how the targets are set or what they are: the fact that there is a specific objective will spur people's performance. Individuals who have specific targets perform better than those who are given vague objectives such as 'do your best'. More than this, Latham and Locke (1979) report both laboratory and field research which shows that people who have challenging targets perform better than people who have moderately difficult or easy targets. However, performance feedback and increased pay seem to lead to improved performance only when these incentives lead individuals to set higher targets. Latham and Locke reach these conclusions.

- Difficult but attainable targets increase the challenge of the job.
- Specific targets make it clear what employees are expected to do.
- Feedback on progress towards targets provides employees with a sense of achievement, recognition and accomplishment.
- Employees can compare their current and past performance and, in some cases, compare themselves with others. This may lead them to greater effort, and to devise better or more creative tactics for attaining their targets.

There is much debate about *how* targets should be set, even though the evidence clearly shows that the important thing is to *set* a target. Research shows that higher production is the result when employees have targets; it does not matter whether the targets are simply assigned or the employees have participated in setting them. On the whole, it seems that participation in setting targets leads to better performance only to the extent that it leads employees to set even higher targets. So, the appropriate method of target-setting will depend very much on the management system and style of the particular organisation. What we do know is that effective performance targets, objectives or indicators have these SMART features: they are S*pecific,* M*easurable,* A*greed,* R*ealistic* and T*ime-framed.*

Specific targets

Effective targets are specific rather than vague and concentrate on the results to be achieved rather than on the activity expected of the employee. Thus, 'to increase sales by 10 per cent' is much more specific than 'to try to improve sales'. It describes the desired outcome, whereas 'try to improve sales' deals only with the employee's effort or input. When the time comes to review the employee's performance, it will be a matter of fact whether sales have increased by 10 per cent. But what can a manager say to the employee who claims to have tried to improve sales, but without result?

Try to find an *accomplishment* verb which can start the target by stating the expected results. Words like *increase, reduce, establish, agree, conduct, provide* and *achieve* describe an expected outcome in action terms, but words like *study, discuss* and *consider* are about the activities or inputs required of the employee in trying to achieve the expected outcome.

Remember that not all targets can be about improving or developing performance. For many people in many positions, the main requirement will be to reach a certain level of performance within a certain time and then maintain it. Setting performance improvement targets in such jobs can be an artificial exercise that compromises the real purpose and potential benefits of performance planning and review.

* *Is this target measurable? Does it tell me precisely what I have to do to succeed?*

Measurable targets

Together with the expected results, effective targets will include the measures or standards to be used in assessing those results. Those measures or standards should be agreed in advance by manager and employee or, at least, the employee should know about and accept the standards or measures. They may be *quantitative*, as in 'increase sales by 10 per cent', or *qualitative*, using a standard or descriptive statement agreed by the manager and employee. Often, qualitative targets can be expressed in quantitative terms, as in 'improve customer satisfaction so that service complaints do not exceed one per week on average'. There is no job in which the desired performance or results cannot be measured in some way.

* *Does the target tell me how the results will be measured?*

Agreed targets

Getting employees' commitment is a key to setting effective targets. Employees should participate fully in the setting of the objectives for their own jobs, and have an opportunity to contribute to planning the objectives of the work group, the department and the organisation as a whole. But people should not be left to set their own targets: each individual's objectives must fit in with those of the wider work group or workplace. How much you involve employees in setting their targets will depend on the organisation's approach to performance management and on its style and culture generally. At the very least, managers should ensure that the person responsible for achieving a particular objective understands and accepts it. Employees will not feel committed to targets that are just handed down to them by management.

* *Am I, and any other people who are involved, committed to the achievement of this target?*

Realistic targets

Targets should be challenging, but not beyond the reasonable reach of the employee. If they are accepted by the employee, moderately difficult targets usually lead to better performance than easy targets. But employees will simply not accept targets that they perceive to be unreasonable or unreachable. They get no sense of achievement either from pursuing targets they can never reach. Similarly, targets that are set too low will not challenge people's capabilities and will have no motivating effect.

Targets are realistic if they are consistent with the organisation's plans and objectives, within the scope of the individual's responsibilities, and within the individual's skills and abilities. Sometimes, individuals or groups have to be dissuaded from taking on objectives which are beyond their capabilities or which cannot be achieved with the available resources.

* *Does this target offer me a challenge? And is there a reasonable chance that I can meet that challenge?*

Time-framed targets

Just as targets should be specific rather than vague, they should also have a time frame or time limit, as in 'increase sales by 10 per cent by the end of the financial year'. If several targets are being set, check that their time spans or completion dates are staggered through the period. For many people, targets will have only limited effect if their completion dates are, say, twelve months away or people might feel unduly pressured if all their targets are due for completion at the same time. Target dates must be realistic: we frequently underestimate how long it will take to complete certain activities, especially if several different objectives have to be achieved within the same period of time.

'Time-framed' should also mean that progress is reviewed regularly. For example, a project targeted for completion by the end of the financial year might have interim reviews scheduled at three-monthly intervals. This ensures that progress is being checked regularly and, if necessary, the completion date can be revised or more resources allocated to the project. However, there is a fine line between reviewing progress towards the achievement of a target and checking up on what the employee is doing. Whether or not you cross that line will be a matter of frequency and timing, and a matter of management style.

As long ago as 1965, American researchers found that short-term target-setting was much more likely to improve performance for process workers and people in similar jobs than an annual review cycle (Meyer et al. 1965). Employees can be vague about annual targets. But if they're in positions where they should understand their long-term objectives, then it's the manager's responsibility to clarify the situation. For many jobs, especially in fast-changing organisations or markets, it might be of more value to discuss specific expectations and set targets frequently rather than set more broadly stated annual targets.

- *When do I need to have this completed? When do we review progress?*

Responsibility levels

In addition to the SMART factors, it is important to check that objectives state the correct level of responsibility for the individual and the job. Many targets, especially in MBO-based systems, tend to overstate both the level of involvement and the level of accountability. If taken literally, these statements could confuse people's perceptions of organisational relationships and responsibilities; if not queried, but accepted in their inaccurate or misleading form, they risk the credibility of the target-setting process.

There are two problems. First, a job description might incorrectly state the job holder's level or area of responsibility. For example, a staff specialist might be described as 'responsible' for certain achievements or actions which are, in fact, the responsibilities of line managers. Staff specialists should be held responsible for the quality and timeliness of the advice and assistance they give, but can hardly be held responsible for how other people act on that advice or assistance. Second, some objectives link 'cause' and 'effect' to an extent that cannot be justified. It is unlikely to be accurate, for example, to write an objective for a despatch assistant that says 'contributes to company profitability by ensuring all deliveries are despatched within 24 hours of order being received'. Getting deliveries despatched on time might contribute to customer satisfaction, for which the despatch assistant might be said to share some responsibility, but it is very remote from company profitability.

Another problem arises when targets or objectives are set because the system requires it. We have seen already that in many jobs, especially in relatively straightforward production, processing or administration roles, the proper objective is to achieve and maintain a specified level of performance. Setting higher targets for these jobs—in terms of more work volume, for example—could be both undesirable and incapable of achievement.

TARGETS FOR MANAGERS

Setting performance targets and standards for managers, especially for chief executives and other top-level managers, presents a special challenge. Boards of directors might agree that top management has a primary responsibility to establish and safeguard the organisation's mission and corporate culture, to develop a strategic direction and approach to the organisation's business, to provide leadership and to build an effective management team. However, those same directors typically judge their top managers on the overall financial performance of the organisation and similar quantitative targets. Not only does this send wrong signals to the management group, it is confusing for the rest of the organisation as well.

Increasingly, there is disagreement about what targets are appropriate for managers. On one side are those who focus their attention on the organisation's 'bottom line', seeing financial results and 'shareholder value'—usually code for a company's current share price, which might not have much to do with value—as the only worthwhile measures of managers' performance. On the other side are those who recognise that, for managers at all levels, leadership and other non-quantitative managerial behaviours are the key to performance for both the organisation and its employees. In a sense, this side of the argument understands that managers' jobs are concerned mainly with making the 'inputs' which allow or encourage—or hinder and block—the organisation from achieving its desired 'outcomes'. They think that managers should be held accountable for their inputs, yet they also understand that the efforts of a single manager are only one part of a complex series of influences on those outcomes.

It can be difficult to assess the qualitative performance of senior executives, especially in a diversified and decentralised organisation. Those who have to review the performance of managers are seldom able to observe them on a consistent or continuous basis. Assessing the true nature of the relationship between managers and their employees, or judging the effectiveness of their team leadership is very difficult unless the performance reviewer is close to the action—and the presence of an outside observer may very well change some aspects of that situation.

Thus, special care is needed when drawing up job descriptions for chief executive and other top management roles and in preparing the 'management' part of job descriptions and performance objectives for other levels of manager. One possible approach, adapted from Burchman and Schneier (1989), is set out in the box below. It is part of the accountability statements and performance indicators for a chief executive position, but can be used as a model for other management roles and positions.

Chief Executive Officer

Accountability: Organises, develops and leads the management team

Element of accountability	Performance indicators
Establishes, evaluates and, as necessary, changes the management structure to improve organisational effectiveness and efficiency.	• Ratio of overhead to operational costs is better than industry norms. • Organisation has fewer management layers than industry norms. • Management structure supports business strategy.
Attracts, selects, develops and retains the best available management talent.	• Voluntary management turnover is below industry norms • Quality of management team, as reflected through appraisal process and financial/non-financial results for each business unit, consistently exceeds standards. • When external recruitment necessary, organisation is consistently able to hire leading candidates. • Management development plans are in place and being implemented for all management positions.

Ensures continuity in the management team through appropriate succession plans.	• Succession plans are in place for all key executive positions. • Organisation is able to fill key positions with quality candidates from within the organisation.
Makes effective use of management team through appropriate delegation and empowerment and involvement in corporate decision-making.	• Decision-making roles for key decisions are set out in writing and understood by those affected. • Decisions are made at the lowest possible organisational level consistent with the risk to the organisation's interests. • Top executives participate actively in corporate decision-making.
Stimulates collaboration and cooperation among members of the management team.	• Potential synergies among business units are identified and exploited. • Where feasible, resources are shared among business units: management succession plans cut across business unit lines; where feasible, duplicate systems have been eliminated; cross-selling is the norm rather than the exception.
Sets clear performance expectations for the management team, provides appropriate feedback and coaching, and acts decisively to replace executives who do not meet requirements.	• A performance management system is in place for top executives. It establishes performance plans in writing and these are formally reviewed at least once a year. The results of performance reviews are reported to the Board. • Non-performing executives have been replaced.

Deming (1986) argued that traditional target-setting is unfair and counterproductive because it uses arbitrary figures—'increase sales by

5 per cent' or 'project to be completed within two months'—without considering whether such targets are necessary, achievable or even meaningful. There is, of course, no excuse for setting targets that are unnecessary, unachievable or meaningless. Deming would have had a stronger case if he'd argued that traditional target-setting tends to concentrate on short-term, quantitative outcomes which can lead managers to ignore longer-term consequences. For example, investment fund managers whose performance is judged according to a quarterly index might expose their clients to high risks in order to boost their short-term performance by a percentage point or two. Or long-term customer relations might be put at risk by a product price rise designed to boost end-of-year sales income figures.

Thus, the challenge in setting objectives for managers is to select the right objectives. Getting a new computer system installed by a target date is pointless if the system doesn't work. A better target would involve getting the system installed and working. But, as Drummond (1993) illustrates, the challenge of target-setting for managers goes even further.

Two local government managers working for different councils were given the task of installing a new contracts management software system. In both cases, the system was 'to be operational by the end of May'. Manager A met the target, insofar as by the end of May the system was installed and working, apart from 'a few teething troubles'.

Manager B, however, reported that a preliminary analysis of costs, organisational requirements and system capability suggested that the proposed software package might not be suitable, and that it would certainly be more expensive to purchase and would require more staff to operate than was originally envisaged.

Who is the better manager, A or B? Manager A has met the target, whereas Manager B appears to be floundering, but is it as simple as that? The 'teething troubles' experienced by Manager A turned out to be identical to the problems identified by Manager B. The difference is that Manager A discovered the snags too late, having already purchased the system. Manager A's predicament resulted not from an act of God, but from failure to manage.

Purchase of computer software is invariably fraught with difficulties. Had Manager A done his job properly he too would have realised this. Nevertheless, having met the target, he will be judged successful. If Manager A is later questioned about the cost of additional hardware and software necessary to render the system fully operational he can claim he was given insufficient time to appraise the system.

Ignoring your inevitable and justifiable reactions about inappropriate specifications and inadequate analysis, which are themselves a result of management failures, this cautionary tale makes two key points. First, managers are often held accountable for results or outcomes and their performance in these areas is typically judged in quantitative terms. Yet managers are generally employed to make inputs to the processes and procedures that other people use to achieve results. In other words, managing is about achieving results through other people. Therefore, if *managers* are to be held accountable for *managing*, we need to be rather more certain just what it is we expect managers to do, what behaviours we expect from them and what we expect to be the outcomes of their managing.

The 'organises, develops and leads the management team' accountability for a chief executive on page 61 is one example of this approach. Here's another example, from a financial services organisation which includes these specific 'people management' functions in its standard performance review format for managers.

- **Managing employees**
  —Accepts accountability for managing people and their performance.
  —Delegates appropriate tasks and assignments to build employees' skills.
  —Encourages teamwork among employees.
- **Developing employees**
  —Encourages employees to recognise and use their potential.
  —Encourages employees to identify their own needs for knowledge and skills.
  —Provides on-job training and coaching for employees.

As another example, the performance planning and review format of a large services company has a special supplementary section for managers. It sets out the main areas of managers' responsibilities as:

- managing work programs and budgets
- managing relations with clients inside and outside the organisation
- managing relations with others inside the organisation
- providing technical and policy guidance to ensure desired results are achieved, and
- managing and developing people.

The first four areas of responsibility are covered in the main section of the manager's performance plan and review, while the 'people management' responsibility is given special treatment. The supplementary form provides five headings to focus managers' attention on the areas of people management where potential benefits are greatest. They are:

- setting priorities and taking decisions
- communicating clear performance expectations and performance feedback
- providing guidance and support to staff on their personal development
- delegating responsibility and encouraging innovation
- fostering cooperation and teamwork within and between sections.

With this approach, the company is seeking to put the focus on those aspects of its managers' behaviour which, it believes, need most attention and which also contribute most to the improved performance of all employees. The company believes that the key to improved management performance is to help its managers understand that what they *do* in the managing role may be more important than what they appear to achieve.

But that doesn't mean that performance targets cannot—or should not—be set for managers. It does suggest, however, that those targets might better be expressed in terms of the behaviours expected of managers. Thus, 'maintaining good relations with employees' might be a reasonable expectation of managers, even though it scarcely meets the SMART test for performance targets. How do you make that target more specific and measurable? One approach is to ask managers what they plan to do to maintain good relations with their employees. A manager who intends to hold regular meetings with employees and their representatives, to act quickly on employee problems or complaints, and to seek advice and assistance from the human resources department when disciplinary action seems to be needed would appear to understand some of the factors that contribute to good employee relations. Those intended actions are both specific and measurable in the sense that the manager can subsequently be asked 'What did you actually do?' A manager who has no specific actions in mind will probably do nothing to maintain good relations with employees; the results may be both regrettable and obvious.

CHAPTER 5

REVIEWING PERFORMANCE

Traditionally, performance appraisal systems have centred on a once-a-year interview between the manager and the employee. That discussion has often been a review of the employee's behavioural traits or personal characteristics. As we have seen in earlier chapters, performance planning and review should be a year-round process and it should focus on performance requirements and achievements, not on the person or personality of the employee.

In other words, the formal performance discussion should spring no surprises. It should be an opportunity for people who work together all the time to take a step back from their day-to-day relationship, to summarise the period just gone and, in the light of that experience and the business or operating objectives of the unit or department, plan for the time or work ahead.

The traditional performance appraisal interview often involves a series of supposedly 'constructive' criticisms of past performance, from which the employee is expected to learn and gain motivation to do better in future. Unfortunately, criticism—even 'constructive' criticism—doesn't have this effect on most people. And because the interview usually focuses on what went wrong, praise has little impact in the performance appraisal interview. Employees see praise simply as wrapping for the criticism which they perceive to be the interview's real purpose.

A once-a-year interview is not the appropriate time to pick up on individual mistakes or incidents of inadequate performance; they should have been dealt with when they happened. Nor, in my view, is it an appropriate time to talk about an employee's future aspirations. It's not the best place or time, nor is the manager necessarily the best person to ask such questions as 'Where would you like to be in five years' time?' The main purpose of the performance discussion is to enable two people who 'contracted' for certain performance to take an overview of the outcomes of that contract, and to agree on what should happen in the time ahead.

Guidelines for effective performance reviews

- Recognise appraisal as one part of a total process of improving performance
- Forms don't matter
- Concentrate on performance rather than personality
- Encourage participation
- Keep appraisal in the hands of management
- Insist on benefits

WHAT PERFORMANCE DO WE REVIEW?

Once the emphasis of performance planning and review shifts from the judgment of people and personalities to the assessment of job-related performance, we have to think about what aspects of performance will be reviewed. This question is more important now that quantitative and numerical performance targets are no longer seen as the only appropriate measures or indicators of effective performance. Obviously, the performance plan set at the beginning of the period or project will provide the main focus or agenda for the performance review. However, in considering how much progress has been made towards achieving the targets set out in the performance plan, we should identify what aspects of them are most important. What matters most?

Is it most important to focus on what is achieved? If so, the performance review and discussion will probably concentrate on items such as deadlines, sales targets and production volume levels. The performance planning and review system will probably be results-orientated (see pages 88–93).

Is what is done most significant? If so, the discussion will examine how the work is being carried out and look at the actual behaviour of the employee on the job. In this case, the performance planning and review system could be based on Behaviourally Anchored Rating Scales (see pages 83–5).

In some cases, what people *are* is critical to job success, so the focus of the review is on relevant personal characteristics and behaviours. These can include an employee's managerial style, the ability to work in a team environment or how good the person is at managing a project. Nevertheless, the emphasis continues to be on the person's behaviour, rather than the person. Here, a competency-based method of assessment would be most appropriate (see pages 93–8).

HOW DO WE REVIEW PERFORMANCE?

There seems to be a never-ending search for an ideal technique for performance review or appraisal. Often, this search is aimed at finding an 'objective' method of measuring or assessing performance. We might ask whether it's ever possible to be objective in management decision-making, or whether the aim is simply to avoid making decisions that are arbitrary, ill-informed, discriminatory or biased. After all, we employ managers, at least in part, for their decision-making abilities; if objectivity were possible and desirable, we would need only to employ operators of objective decision-making systems—in other words, robots!

Unfortunately, the search for objectivity can lead us to design performance review systems that seem to encourage a mechanistic selection from a range of given options rather than real substantive input and decision-making from managers. That lack of involvement and contribution might be another reason why many managers dislike the performance appraisal systems they are required to use.

The choice of performance review methods ranges from simple ranking—which is concerned more with comparing employees than assessing their performance—through to complex procedures like Behaviourally Anchored Rating Scales and assessment centres. Clearly, no technique will suit all organisations and all circumstances, and organisations may have to use different techniques in different situations or for different purposes.

However, some methods have very limited use in performance management and can be safely left to one side. *Forced distribution*, for example, calls for all employees—quite large numbers are needed to ensure validity—to be distributed in proper statistical array over a normal or bell-shaped curve. Large United States corporations have been reported using forced distribution to select employees for lay-off in times of business downturn: the lowest 10 per cent or 20 per cent on the bell curve are easy candidates for termination (see pages 72–3).

The real disadvantage of forced distribution, like many simple ranking techniques, is that it compares the performance of one employee with the performance of others. Performance is not necessarily reviewed against either performance standards or performance targets. In other words, you know who performed best and who performed worst, but you don't necessarily know whether anyone met the desired performance standard or target.

Other techniques are useful for some purposes, but not others. For example, Behaviourally Anchored Rating Scales (BARS) have specific application in employee development, and *paired comparisons* can be helpful in making promotion decisions. But they are probably less useful—and less practicable for most organisations in the case of BARS—in performance planning and review.

Discrimination issues are a further consideration. All reviews inevitably contain some element of personal judgment, but this should be only a minor feature. In the United States, for example, courts have held that personal judgments must be rational and well-considered and, preferably, based on previously established and well-publicised standards (Townley 1990). Those courts have also rejected the paired comparison method where managers are asked to choose which of two employees is 'better' without objectively defining 'better'. Similarly, subjective criteria such as 'adaptability' and 'general intelligence' have been questioned as open to bias. Performance planning and review systems that focus on actual job content and actual job behaviour, preferably with predetermined performance standards or targets, are more likely to avoid the problems of bias and discrimination.

PERFORMANCE REVIEW METHODS

All performance review methods have their advantages and disadvantages: the aim should be to select one that meets the needs and circumstances of the organisation and its employees, remembering that the best solution might involve combining two or more different techniques. Consider these issues:

- What resources does the organisation have available for the development and implementation of its performance management system? What resources is it willing to commit—especially cost and time—to this process?
- What are the objectives of the system? Is the emphasis to be on judging past performance, planning future performance or assessing employees' potential?
- What are the organisation's human resources and other management strategies, policies and programs? How will the performance planning and review system fit into the overall approach to performance and people management?
- Which employees will be covered by the new system? What is the nature of their work, their working environment and their working relationships?
- How large and sophisticated is the organisation? What does that suggest about the degree of system and sophistication that would be appropriate for performance planning and review?

- What are the organisation's training and development philosophies and programs? How are they to be linked to the performance planning and review system?
- What experience does the organisation have of performance planning and review? How do people feel about such systems? What expertise can the organisation draw on?

Reliability and validity

'Reliability' and 'validity' have special meanings when we're discussing the usefulness and effectiveness of performance assessment or measurement instruments. *Reliability* describes how well an instrument produces consistent data over time. In other words, will it describe the same behaviour in the same terms on different occasions, or give the same performance the same rating at different times? *Validity* deals with what an instrument or method measures and how well it makes that measurement. In simple terms, does this approach measure or assess what it intends to measure or assess?

COMPARISON OR RANKING METHODS

Comparison or ranking methods require each person—or some characteristic of a person or a person's performance—to be compared with every other employee, with the results then being used to produce a rank order for all the employees. These methods are simple and easily understood, quick and inexpensive to implement and can achieve relatively high reliability, but they are not often used for performance planning and review. There are some major problems.

Comparisons are usually made on the basis of a single behavioural dimension (e.g. 'reliability') or job-related characteristic (e.g. 'product knowledge') or some overall assessment (e.g. 'value to the organisation'). Unless these descriptors are given specific definitions, there is a risk that different reviewers will apply different standards in assessing relative worth, and the rank order will lack a defensible rationale. One person might be ranked higher or lower than another, yet this ranking tells us nothing substantive about the performance of either of them. Both employees might be brilliant performers, or it could be that neither of them is meeting minimum performance standards—but ranking by itself will not tell us that. Similarly, it is difficult to use ranking methods for comparisons between groups of employees, because the highest ranking person in one department might be only 'average' in another part of the organisation. And, because rankings don't produce specific information about an employee's performance strengths and weaknesses, they are not much use for feedback and development. An employee doesn't learn very much from being told that he or she is better or worse than someone else!

In summary, despite the attractions of simplicity, comparison or ranking methods have major disadvantages for performance management (although they can be useful for other purposes, such as selection decisions).

- They assume that the employees who are ranked all undertake the same kinds of work, which is seldom the case, especially in smaller organisations.
- They are cumbersome when large numbers of employees are involved, or when more than one manager has to contribute to the ranking process, or when a number of characteristics need to be ranked.
- They rank people in order, but do not show how much better one person is than another or whether any of the employees actually reach the expected standards.
- They do not provide reasons for the rankings.
- They are subject to bias and discrimination on the part of those who decide the rankings.

Straight ranking

Employees are simply ranked in order according to the manager's assessment of their overall performance or some aspect of that performance, or on their value to the organisation. Obviously, ranking becomes more difficult as the number of employees increases. Another problem is that managers can avoid assessing actual performance and can even avoid specifying what is being assessed. In practice, managers will rank 'people' rather than their 'performance' or 'effectiveness'.

Alternation ranking

The names of all the employees to be ranked are listed alphabetically. The reviewer then selects the 'best' and 'worst' employee—on the basis of overall performance or using a characteristic such as 'effectiveness'—

and shifts their names to the top and bottom positions on a new list. The next 'best' and 'worst' employees are then selected from the remaining names on the original list and shifted to the next available slots at the top and bottom of the new list. This process continues until all names have been shifted. Of course, the new rank order of employees simply identifies each person as better or worse than the others. It does not tell us anything substantive about the employees' relative importance.

Paired comparisons

Each employee is compared with every other employee in the group, one at a time, either on overall performance or on a particular aspect of the job. If employee A is considered 'better' than employee B, A is given two points. If the employees are considered 'equally good', A gets one point. No points are scored if A is rated 'worse' than B. When every pair has been compared, the scores for each employee are added up and arranged in rank order.

Forced distribution or ranking

This technique is so named because it requires appraisers to assign a set proportion of employees to each of several performance categories. For example, the requirement might be for 10 per cent of employees to be rated 'high' performers, 20 per cent 'above average', 40 per cent 'average', 20 per cent 'below average' and 10 per cent 'low' performers.

Supporters of forced ranking say that it makes managers take tough decisions that would otherwise be avoided. And some organisations (see box opposite) see it as a way to a continuously improving workforce. But there are problems.

As with all comparison and ranking methods, forced distribution does not determine whether an employee can do the job to the required standard, or if the employee is achieving the job targets. Similarly, some employees must always end up in the lower-performing or unsatisfactory categories, even if they are performing to the required standards or levels. Moreover, it is always possible that the low performers in one business unit or department will be making a more valuable contribution than the high performers somewhere else in the organisation.

Finally, forced ranking can set up unhealthy internal competition and weaken team work if individuals try to protect their own positions at the expense of their colleagues. There is also a risk that terminations based on forced ranking will lead to unfair dismissal claims against the employer.

Rank and yank

Time magazine (11 June 2001) reported that forced ranking appraisal systems have spread to about 20 per cent of US companies. Sun Microsystems, for example, ranks its employees into three groups. The top 20 per cent are rated 'superior', the next 70 per cent are 'standard' and, at the bottom, there is a 10 per cent band of 'underperformers'. The underperformers are told frankly that they must improve and are provided with one-on-one coaches. CEO Scott McNealy tells his executives that the underperformers must be 'loved to death'. Another example is Microsoft, which annually weeds out about 5 per cent of its workforce through its employee appraisal system.

Ford Motor Company has been taken to court over its performance management process, which ranks employees on a bell curve. Introduced in June 2000, the system provided for 10 per cent of the company's managers to be assigned the highest A grade, 80 per cent to be given a B grade and 10 per cent graded C. Those who were graded C would be ineligible for pay increases or bonuses. Two Cs in a row would qualify a manager for demotion or dismissal. The plaintiffs claimed that Ford was using the system to get rid of older managers, because the performance evaluation criteria included items such as willingness to learn new activities, upgrade skills and become involved in change initiatives.

One of the leading practitioners of forced ranking was Enron Corporation, the Texas energy trader which collapsed in 2001. Before its demise, Enron was held up as proof that 'rank and yank' was the future for all performance appraisals, and that it had produced 'a hotbed of overachievers' for the company.

STANDARDS-BASED REVIEWS

Like comparison or ranking methods, standards-based review methods concentrate on an employee's characteristics or traits, rather than the person's actual performance or behaviour. There are two main groups of standards-based reviews:

- The reviewer decides whether the employee has a certain trait or characteristic: the answer is a simple 'Yes' or 'No'. *Critical incidents*, *checklists* and *forced choice* are some of the methods in this group.

- The reviewer assesses the extent to which the employee has a certain trait or characteristic. The response is usually plotted on a *rating scale*.

Some standards-based review methods are quite simple and may not have much validity; others are highly sophisticated and systematic, which may in itself be a barrier to their widespread adoption.

Critical incidents

Over a period of time, the manager keeps a record of on-job incidents or behaviour as examples of effective or ineffective behaviour. This diary is used as a factual background for the year-end review or performance discussion. This approach sounds straightforward but is only reliable if the critical success factors for the job have been identified in advance. To do this, managers are asked to provide examples of when employees were particularly effective or ineffective in their jobs, and these incidents are then grouped into behavioural categories. As many as a hundred incidents might be needed to produce ten general categories for a particular job. The manager then notes down any positive or negative on-job incidents that occur in each of these categories.

It is difficult for managers to record a representative sample of employees' work behaviour. It is more likely that they will note down 'major' incidents, regardless of whether they represent 'good' or 'bad' behaviour. At the same time, managers will almost inevitably include their judgments of the employee in the diary, whereas this approach calls for the record only to describe behaviour. In any case, we cannot be very confident that watching a person work will lead us to valid conclusions about that person's behaviour. It is also time-consuming for managers and can lead some employees to believe they are being closely and continuously supervised, or spied on.

Critical incidents interviewing—when employees are asked when their job seemed to be going particularly well or particularly badly, or when they were feeling satisfied or dissatisfied—can be useful for job analysis and for determining the main success factors in a job.

Essays and *narrative appraisals* are similar in approach to the critical incidents method. The manager writes a report on the employee's performance, covering any matters considered important or significant. Typically, managers will be asked to discuss employees' strengths and weaknesses, their potential and their overall performance. They may be given a series of broad questions to consider—such as 'What are the employee's main achievements this year?'—to ensure that there is some consistency or standardisation in the reports. The essay approach can be used as a self-appraisal technique, but is most commonly used in conjunction with other methods as a summary device. The obvious problems with narrative methods are questions of comprehensiveness and difficulties of bias. In addition, many managers are not good at written expression.

Checklists

To develop a checklist for performance review, statements about employee characteristics or behaviours in a job are gathered from people who know the job well, and then assessed and weighted according to how favourable or unfavourable they are for effective performance. The reviewing manager is given the list, without the weightings shown, and asked to indicate whether the employee does or does not engage in the particular behaviours. That assessment may be made on a simple 'Yes' or 'No' basis (as in the example below) by noting how frequently the employee engages in the behaviour on a scale from, say, 5 equals *Always* through 3 equals *Sometimes* to 1 equals *Never*.

Despite its apparent simplicity, the checklist approach requires you to have a very close understanding of a job and its key success factors if the list of performance criteria is to be validly selected and weighted. To check the reliability of the assessments, the same or very similar questions may be asked in different ways, as is the case with Questions 7 and 10 in this example.

Performance checklist: Retail sales assistant

Employee's name:
Reviewed by: *Date:*

Does this employee	Yes	No
1. arrive for work on time?		
2. have good selling skills?		
3. have good product knowledge?		
4. handle cash according to procedures?		
5. handle cheques according to procedures?		
6. handle credit cards according to procedures?		
7. respond politely to customers?		
8. leave customers waiting?		
9. restock shelves when necessary?		
10. use bad language with customers?		

Forced choice

This is a development of the checklist approach. Managers are given lists of employee behaviours and asked to select those that are applicable most and least to individual staff members. The statements are worded so that, overall, they appear equally favourable or unfavourable, to encourage the manager to make a choice on a descriptive rather than judgmental basis. The manager's choices are 'scored' according to a predetermined weighting which the manager does not see, and then distributed for the whole work group on a normal curve.

Forced choice comparison

Which of these statements is most like and least like the employee?

Most	*Least*	
[ ]	[ ]	Reports are completed on time
[ ]	[ ]	Gets along well with work colleagues
[ ]	[ ]	Fails to prepare for presentations
[ ]	[ ]	Considers ideas from other people
[ ]	[ ]	Gives credit to others who perform well
[ ]	[ ]	Gets upset under pressure of deadlines

In more sophisticated forced choice systems, list items are chosen according to two indices: a *discrimination* index which measures whether the item differentiates between successful and unsuccessful performance, and a *desirability* index which measures whether the item is a favourable or unfavourable statement to make about an employee. Done properly, forced choice is a very complex approach that requires expert advice and assistance and is thus time-consuming and expensive to introduce.

Generally, forced choice is not popular with managers. They want to know what performance rating they are giving their employees, and they cannot use the statements to provide feedback. And neither managers nor employees have much chance of understanding the complex methodology.

Rating scales

Graphic, or linear, rating scales are the most popular of the standards-based approaches to performance appraisal or review and, in some form, probably the most frequently used approach. They are readily adapted to suit specific jobs and organisations, and there is virtually no limit to the aspects of person or performance that can be rated.

In simple terms, rating scales require the reviewer to rate the employee's performance in an absolute sense, not in comparison to other employees. Employees can be rated on virtually any trait or characteristic or dimension of performance or behaviour.

Rating systems are easily constructed. The characteristics to be assessed are chosen and each step on the scale is given a brief description in terms of quantity or quality. All the rater has to do is choose the statement that best describes the employee. In more complex systems, the various elements may be weighted so that the final rating summarises the employee's overall worth in terms of the organisation's goals or objectives.

The simplest methods provide a rating scale—Excellent 5 4 3 2 1 Poor, for example—but no more information than that. The rating scales at the top of Figure 5.1 (page 78) provide little information on the dimension to be rated and no definition of the various points along the scale. Lower down, the scales offer some definition of the dimension to be rated and this gives some meaning to the points on the scale.

It might seem reasonable to assume that a simple five-point rating scale would be less reliable than a seven-point scale with detailed descriptions of each point on the scale, but this is not necessarily so. Wexley and Klimowski (1984) found that more detailed descriptions do not produce better ratings than simple 'High–Low' or 'Yes–No' scales. Similarly, Matell and Jacoby (1972) tell us there is no relationship between the number of points on a scale and its reliability or validity, provided there are five or more points on the scale. However, it seems that raters find it difficult to make real distinctions where there are more than seven points on the scale. Some organisations use scales that have an even number of points, the aim being to prevent managers from avoiding a decision by taking the middle ground.

Although rating scales are simple to construct, understand and use, there are significant problems.

- The simpler forms of rating scale do not give reviewers any guidance on the content or standard of the characteristics to be rated, and leave them to decide both the absolute and relative merit of terms like *Excellent* and *Poor*. As a result, ratings are essentially subjective.
- Making distinctions between a 2 and a 3 on a five-point rating scale, or between an 8 and a 9 on an eleven-point scale is difficult for most managers, and probably doesn't mean much anyway.

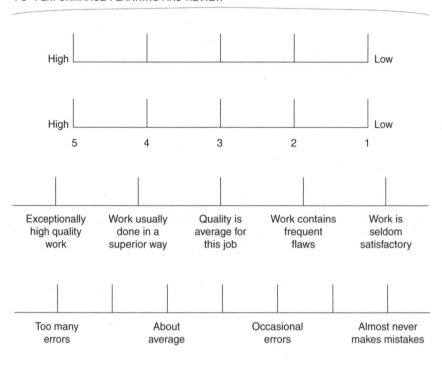

Performance factors	Performance grade			
	Consistently superior	Sometimes superior	Consistently average	Consistently unsatisfactory
Quality Accuracy Economy Neatness				

1	2	3	4	5	6	7	8	9	10	11	12	13	14	15	16	17	18	19	20
Poor					Below average					Average					Above average				

Judge the amount of scrap; consider the general care and accuracy of the employee's work; also consider the inspection record.

Poor 1–6,   Average 7–8,   Good 19–25 _____

FIGURE 5.1   GRAPHIC RATING SCALES: EXAMPLES RELATING TO QUALITY OF WORK

- Rating scales lack flexibility in one key respect. Not all the characteristics of a job are equally important, and certain characteristics are more important for some jobs than for others. Without complicated weighting formulas, rating scales cannot recognise these differences.
- Ratings can be given easily enough for individual characteristics or dimensions, but it is more difficult to turn these into a valid or useful overall assessment.
- Rater error is a problem, especially the *halo effect* where one attribute or incident dominates the overall rating. Managers seem to find it difficult to spread their ratings across the entire scale, leading to the *central tendency* problem where ratings are bunched around the middle of the scale, or a *skewed distribution* where all the ratings are too high or too low. Rating errors are discussed in detail on page 98–101.

Ratings based on more, rather than less information, probably help managers when it comes to making performance assessments and should contribute to more descriptive and helpful feedback for employees.

To overcome the problems of simple rating scales, organisations often provide detailed statements of the performance ratings to be used or the performance factors or job behaviours to be assessed, or both. The personal development review used by one bank, for example, lists twelve job functions on which employees are to be assessed. Five of those functions are used in the extract shown in Figure 5.2.

Each function's 'definition' is followed by two or three descriptive statements which help managers and employees to understand what performance is expected or desired. But, before they attempt to agree on how well the employee has performed in each functional area, the manager and the employee must agree on the importance of that function for the job overall. It is important to also note that the employee is required to make a self-appraisal before discussing the ratings with the manager.

A computer services organisation provides a more detailed guide for its seven-point performance rating system (see box on page 81). Note that these descriptions refer to the skills and abilities of the employee— and thus to the employee's potential future performance—as well as to that person's current actual performance on the job.

One Bank
Personal Development Review

1. Self-review
Before the review discussion, the employee should assess each of the job functions for both *importance* and *performance* and enter those ratings in the appropriate columns. Descriptions for the importance and performance ratings are set out here.

Importance ratings

2 A *key requirement* for the job to be performed effectively.

1 A *standard requirement* for the job to be done.

0 Job function *not relevant* to this position. Do not assign a performance rating.

Performance ratings

4 Results achieved *consistently exceed* the requirements of the job.

3 Results achieved *consistently meet* the requirements of the job and *exceed* requirements in some areas.

2 Results achieved *overall meet* the requirements of the job.

1 Results achieved *do not meet* the requirements of the job.

2. Review discussion
During the review discussion, the manager and the employee compare their responses and attempt to reach agreement on the ratings for each job function.

Job functions	Importance ratings		Performance ratings	
	Employee's rating	Manager's rating	Employee's rating	Manager's rating
1. Builds effective working relationships • Encourages people to work together • Demonstrates commitment to supporting management decisions • Provides support to others when needed				
2. Uses problem-solving abilities • Responds quickly and decisively to problems • Observes and identifies problem areas • Plans ahead to avoid problems in known areas				
3. Shows initiative and resourcefulness • Seeks opportunities to participate in new initiatives • Looks for challenges and gets involved in new areas • Thinks beyond the obvious and seeks opportunities in new work methods or business				
4. Has effective oral communication skills • Presents verbal information clearly and concisely • Actively listens to and considers what others are saying • Presents sound reasoning, enabling others to understand a point of view				
5. Communicates effectively in writing • Prepares written material carefully and concisely • Written material presents a logical sequence of ideas and events				

FIGURE 5.2 EXTRACT FROM A PERSONAL DEVELOPMENT REVIEW

Computer Company

Performance ratings

1. Outstanding
A clearly outstanding key employee who consistently performs all the job requirements with the highest degree of skill and judgment, and with an unusually high level of accomplishment on all the stated job objectives.

2. Superior
This employee consistently exceeds all the stated job requirements. The employee displays a very good all-round level of effectiveness and demonstrates abilities beyond those required in the present position.

3. Very good
This employee consistently achieves an above average standard on all the more important job objectives. The employee readily accepts responsibilities, sometimes beyond the level required in the present position.

4. Fully proficient
This type of employee is a fully competent member of staff who consistently and completely achieves the required standard of the job as defined by the job description, and meets all the job objectives with minimum supervision. Could accept some additional responsibilities in certain circumstances.

5. Mostly proficient
This employee gives an adequate performance against targets. However, achievement on the most important objective(s) could have been better.

6. Improvement required
This employee's performance is not always up to the required standard. There is room for improvement on several important objectives. This is an employee from whom more can be expected based on previous experience and performance. This employee requires definite corrective training.

7. Unsatisfactory
The zone for those whose performance is not meeting the required standard. They must be counselled and, if they do not respond, must be separated from the company.

Computer Company's descriptions apply to experienced staff—that is, to employees who can reasonably be expected to perform to the expected levels or standards. With minor changes, the 'Unsatisfactory' description could be used as a provisional zone for inexperienced newcomers, and 'Mostly proficient' and 'Improvement required' could be used as progression zones for staff in training.

With most rating scales, the score for a fully competent performer comes in the middle of the range. Given that the definition of fully competent performer is usually something like 'performs all the key requirements of the job to the required standards'—in other words, fully competent performers are those who do what they are employed to do—we need to think about the impact on motivation of being rated only in the middle of the scale.

Some organisations overcome this problem by having only three categories of performance: performance that exceeds the requirements of the position; performance that meets those requirements; and performance that falls below the required levels or standards. They recognise that some employees will achieve or contribute beyond the requirements of their jobs, but acknowledge that the basic objective is to have everyone achieve the 'fully competent' performance level. In addition, as shown in the panel below, this 'new' approach to ratings focuses on performance standards: traditional ratings often include words or phrases which imply judgment.

Traditional ratings	'New' ratings
Distinguished	Exceeds standards
Commendable	
Competent	Meets standards
Fair	
Marginal	Does not meet standards

Other standards-based methods have been developed to address the inherent limitations of rating scales. Typically, these methods separate the observation of employee behaviour from its evaluation, and are careful to consider only those aspects of performance or behaviour that are valid to the particular job or organisation. As a result, these methods need significant investments of time and expertise and are very costly to design, implement and manage.

Behaviourally Anchored Rating Scales

The BARS technique aims to overcome the problems of graphic or linear rating scales by replacing the manager's role as judge with that of the objective observer of behaviour. With BARS, the points or *anchors* along the scale are marked by descriptive statements of various levels of performance or *behaviour* which apply to a particular job or an aspect of a job—hence these rating scales are referred to as *behaviourally anchored*.

BARS are attractive in terms of validity, despite somewhat mixed research evidence, but they are complex to develop and implement, and thus beyond the time and money resources of most organisations. Perhaps the main advantage lies with the potential for BARS to encourage more objective assessments, avoiding bias and other common rating errors.

There is also a clear linkage from job descriptions and performance expectations to the BARS format. In other words, reviewers are more likely to make accurate performance assessments if they know in advance what kinds of behaviour are relevant to that performance and its assessment.

To start developing BARS, you gather instances and descriptions of behaviours that lead to effective and ineffective job performance. These are then grouped and written up as performance dimensions for the job or job activity, and assigned a place on a continuum of performance from, for example, 'Unsatisfactory' to 'Outstanding'. These statements are specific to the organisation, the occupation and the job—and this is what makes BARS different from rating scales that use generalised statements or descriptions. BARS concentrate on describing actual job activities and try to avoid quantitative assessments and numerical scores. For this reason, BARS are well suited for reviews for employee development. However, the reviewer needs to have a detailed knowledge of the content of each job.

Schneier and Beatty (1979) provide an example of a Behaviourally Anchored Rating Scale for a specialised machine operation (see box on page 84). It clearly shows how much analysis and preparation the BARS technique requires, as well as the degree of job knowledge needed by both the job analyst and the person who conducts the performance review. In addition, the reviewer would need to have observed the employee on this operation sufficiently often and closely to make a valid and representative assessment of the person's work and behaviour overall.

Behaviourally Anchored Rating Scale

Job dimension: Centrifuge operation

This operator could be expected to:

[7]   vary the centrifuge speed to obtain the best speed for unfamiliar material, constantly monitor evenness of cake

[6]   contact superiors immediately when material does not spin, install bags correctly and quickly, wash cake evenly and completely

[5]   determine correct rate of spin by material appearance, not wash product over basket, always check effluents for solids when starting to spin

[4]   dig out cakes too slowly, load properly but incorrectly judge amount in centrifuge versus amount in pot to obtain correct number of spins, never try to spin without turning on pump, occasionally let cakes run down too long, cause centrifuge to wobble resulting in uneven wet cake

[3]   wash cake at such a speed that only part of the cake gets washed, forget to blow down hose from bottom of pot after loading each spin

[2]   select wrong washing material, forget to place honey cart under centrifuge when digging it out, run effluent over top of bag, overrun centrifuge, or overrun surge tank

[1]   forget to turn on centrifuge pump or open proper outlet valves, frequently tear bags or not report holes in them until end of shift.

Another example—this time for an Accounts Officer in a large service organisation—shows a more generic approach to the development of BARS (see box opposite). The job dimension used in this example is only one of the eight dimensions for this position, indicating how much work is needed to develop comprehensive BARS for an entire department, business unit or organisation.

Behaviourally Anchored Rating Scale

Job title	Accounts Officer
Job holder	....
Job dimension	01 Knowledge of accounting systems, guidelines and policies

Read these descriptions carefully and then choose the one which best describes the employee's job performance.

Outstanding	Can always answer client queries correctly. Wide and detailed knowledge of all accounts guidelines, policies, etc. Actively seeks new knowledge and skills, anticipates new developments. May suggest improvements to systems, etc.
Competent	Has all the knowledge of current systems, etc to produce required outputs. Keeps up to date with new systems, etc.
Unacceptable	Makes incorrect payments and supplies wrong information to clients about policy, etc. Unable or unwilling to update skills and knowledge.

For performance review purposes, this organisation uses two additional intermediate categories: *Above Requirements* is positioned between *Outstanding* and *Competent*, and *Marginal or Trainee* lies between *Competent* and *Unacceptable*. The intermediate categories are not given descriptors and managers are left to interpret them as they wish. Of course, they could be defined but that would add to the workload.

This is a major difficulty with BARS. The performance dimensions can only be indicative of probable types of behaviour, because it would be virtually impossible for most organisations to develop comprehensive descriptions of all aspects of performance. This means that reviewers are left to make their own judgments about where other types of behaviour should fit on a scale.

Behavioural Observation Scales

Behavioural Observation Scales (BOS) can be seen as a simple form of BARS, although it is really more a combination of rating scale and checklist. Job analysis data is used to identify those employee behaviours that are important to effective job performance, but the behaviours are described more generally than in the case of BARS. The scales can be used across a range of jobs and there is less need for detailed knowledge or observation on the part of the reviewer.

After observing the employee's behaviour for a reasonable or representative time, the reviewer assesses that behaviour—typically according to its frequency or extent or standard—on a given scale. As with BARS, the accuracy of assessment is increased because the reviewer knows what behaviour to look for, and the requirement to keep a written record of those behaviours helps to make the assessment more representative and objective. But, again like BARS, the development and implementation of BOS is time-consuming and expensive if the identification of the key behavioural dimensions is done systematically. Thus, BOS is usually suited only to larger organisations.

But, as the example on page 87 shows, BOS descriptions can be much less job-specific than BARS and can be developed with much less intensive or systematic information-gathering. Of course, as with BARS, care is needed to ensure that the chosen behavioural dimensions are those of greatest importance to effective job performance. And, again like BARS, comparisons between employees are difficult. The main value of BOS might be to identify development needs and to indicate where changes in behaviour would be appropriate.

There are clear advantages in giving definitions to the numerical points on the scale:

- It enhances the consistency and comparability of the ratings that different managers give different employees.
- It enables a group of employees to be categorised—for training, rewards, promotion or some other purpose—according to their performance.
- It can help to overcome any potential for competitiveness between managers and employees in the review process.
- It enables reasonably reliable comparisons to be made within and between groups of employees.

Behavioural Observation Scale

Job title   Accounts Officer
Job holder   ....
Job dimension   Team membership

Please rate the behaviour of the job holder using this scale:

5 = almost always (more than 90% of the time)
4 = frequently (80–90%)
3 = sometimes (65–80%)
2 = seldom (50–65%)
1 = almost never (less than 50%)

Strongly energetic and proactive team member
    5   4   3   2   1

Positively leads and supports other team members
    5   4   3   2   1

Tolerates others and their views and is patient with them
    5   4   3   2   1

Plays full and balanced role in work and discussions of team
    5   4   3   2   1

Provides other team members with full information
    5   4   3   2   1

Puts team's work and priorities ahead of own interests and concerns
    5   4   3   2   1

There is another example of a BOS on the next page. It is presented in a different format, and with space for the reviewer to offer specific assessments based on actual observations. This approach has three advantages:

- It gives reviewers a clear idea of what behaviours to look for;
- It increases the likelihood of consistent reviewing across the organisation; and
- It signals to employees what behaviours are expected and valued by the organisation.

Interpersonal skills

Ability to lead, develop and assess employees' performance fairly and effectively, and provide helpful insights and guidance on how to undertake their work activities.

1	**Not ready.** Fails to provide employees with insights on how to undertake their activities; unable to motivate employees to complete tasks; fails to notice when employees need help.
2	**Acceptable.** Consistently shows new employees how to undertake their activities; usually notices if employees need help; provides useful feedback when asked.
3	**Very strong.** Willingly provides guidance to all employees; always available to answer questions; willingly provides very effective feedback to employees.

Write two clear statements for this employee on this competency: One should represent overall performance; one should be a specific example of behaviour you have observed.

....
....
....
....
....
....
....
....

RESULTS-ORIENTED REVIEWS

Performance reviews based on the planning and achieving of specific results are the main alternative to ranking and rating methods. They are based on two ideas.

- People who clearly understand what they are trying to achieve have a better chance of achieving it.
- Progress or improvements in performance can only be measured or assessed in terms of the progress or improvements that people are trying to make.

Management by Objectives

Management by Objectives (MBO) is the best known of the results-oriented methods of performance planning and review and, in some form, probably the most frequently used approach to performance planning and review. Indeed, you might ask if there's any other way to manage, especially if you accept the definition of management as achieving results through people. MBO has been a feature of organisational life since it was popularised in the 1950s by Peter Drucker, John Humble and others as a replacement for the traditional bureaucratic or job-holding approach to employment.

In simple terms, MBO is a target-setting or results-oriented approach to performance management. It recognises that employees perform better when they have targets, and even better when they have participated in setting those targets.

Job analysis is used to produce a job description that sets out the principal accountabilities or key results areas of the job: in other words, the desired outcomes. In this way, the traditional lists of tasks and duties, or inputs, give way to brief statements of expected results in each area of a job. In turn, these are translated into specific targets to be achieved over a particular time period.

While this approach is readily applied to jobs in, say, production or sales—where specifying targets and measuring performance in quantifiable terms is relatively straightforward—it can be more difficult in roles where quality is more important than quantity, or where the prime purpose is to provide support or service to others. In these cases, the challenge is to determine the real reasons for the job's existence and just what is expected of the job holder.

Once the main areas of accountability for a position have been defined and understood, the key to successful MBO, or any other results-oriented method of performance review, lies in the setting of targets or objectives. As we saw in Chapter 4, targets should be SMART—Specific, Measurable, Agreed, Realistic and Time-framed. At a later stage, it is important also to decide how the targets are to be achieved, and this discussion of *how* might take the manager and the employee as long as it takes to set the actual targets. Thus, MBO is a useful way of clarifying job requirements and sharing the mutual expectations of managers and their staff. The agreement of specific work objectives—or performance planning—is a logical starting point for the subsequent performance review.

Designing forms for performance planning and review under MBO can be surprisingly uncomplicated. All a form needs is space for the manager and the employee to note what they agree to be the job's key areas, the targets they set for each of these areas and, for later use, how well the targets were met. Unfortunately, many organisational systems use very complex, and sometimes multi-purpose, forms. At best, these are confusing to the managers and employees who have to use them; at worst, completing the form, rather than planning or reviewing performance, becomes the main objective of the exercise.

MBO has some disadvantages as a method of performance planning and review.

- It has an implicit, sometimes quite explicit, *reward–punishment psychology*.
- Those who achieve the agreed targets are likely to be rewarded with increased pay or promotion, while those who do not attain their objectives are seen to have failed and may be penalised accordingly.
- The setting of targets for improved performance often concentrates on a few major objectives, neglecting those areas of the job where only consistency and continuity are needed. Moreover, it is very difficult to set measurable objectives for some key job areas, such as the 'managing people' part of every manager's job.
- MBO often focuses on the number of objectives to be achieved, or the 'quantity' of the performance or outcome that is to be attained; in some situations, the level of difficulty or the quality of the results might be more important. This focus on numbers attracts criticism of MBO from, for example, the advocates of total quality management.

Partly for these reasons, organisations which base performance planning and review on *how* results are achieved take a different view on defining results. They look for alternatives to numerical measures and quantifiable targets. Obviously, results and expectations can be expressed in many ways, although they should always be capable of being measured in some way. How that measurement will be done should be agreed when the performance plans are set.

The major advantage of results-oriented approaches is that it is not difficult to determine whether, or to what extent, targets have been achieved—provided they have been clearly stated and the data for measuring results is available. There is less focus on judging employees' traits or characteristics and more opportunity for objective discussion of how and why targets were achieved or not achieved. Employees are more able and willing to participate in this kind of discussion, and less likely to adopt the defensive stance characteristic of employees who are called in to hear, and perhaps comment on, the manager's appraisal of them.

Of course, results-oriented systems are not very useful for making comparisons between people. In my view, this is not a major disadvantage in a performance management system. What we should want to compare is the *actual performance* of the employee with the *performance targets* that person agreed with the manager. Different individuals have different job priorities, bring different skills and talents to their jobs, and are subject to different circumstances and pressures during the performance period. These factors all make comparisons of the performance of individuals rather risky. It can be done using broad terms, such as *consistently exceeded job requirements* or *did not meet job requirements*, but we need to ask how helpful such judgments are in managing and developing employee performance.

There is another danger in making comparisons between employees using results-based assessments. Performance planning usually concentrates on areas of the job where improvement or development is desired or required, and performance targets are set for those areas. It would be very unusual to set targets in areas where performance already meets or exceeds expectations. Subsequently, the review of performance will focus on the targets that were set, and may pass over other areas of the job where there were no specific targets because performance was satisfactory.

And there's another problem in comparing employees. A high performer might agree to a small number of very challenging targets in a performance plan, while an average performer, or a person new to the job, could agree to a larger number of less challenging targets. At the end of the performance period, the high performer might have only partially achieved the very difficult targets, whereas the lower performers could have far exceeded their more modest goals. On most scoring or rating systems, comparisons would not recognise these different circumstances and an overall assessment could produce an unfair result.

Similarly, in making overall performance assessments, we should ensure that all aspects of performance are taken into account and not just those areas where targets for improvement or development were set. Not all jobs require that people perform more or better. Virtually every organisation depends on a core of people whom it expects to attain and maintain a certain level or standard of performance. They are as valuable, and as deserving of fair performance reviews, as those employees who constantly need to improve their performance.

Organisations commonly combine various methods and techniques in developing performance planning and review systems. For example, a system might usefully combine MBO, which is a way to determine *what* an employee is expected to do, with behavioural ratings concerned with *how* an employee carries out job requirements or behaves on the job.

Figure 5.3 shows in outline form how a combined job description and performance plan can set out both performance targets and the criteria to be used in assessing how well those targets are met. In addition, because this is a management position, the plan sets out the behavioural criteria (selected from a much longer list) that are to be used in assessing this job holder's performance as a manager.

Defining behavioural criteria

As we have seen, there can be dangers in using personal or personality traits and characteristics in the assessment or review process. The most obvious risk arises when behavioural criteria are simply listed in very brief terms, as they are in Figure 5.3, and are open to interpretation by individual managers and employees. It is useful, at least, to give managers

Position	Operations Manager		
Job holder	A B Carter		
Date	January 2003		
Job purpose	To plan, direct and control the regional and branch operations to ensure that the annual profit and growth objectives are achieved within budget guidelines.		

Key results areas	Measures and reports	Standards and targets	Timing
Direct regional operations to ensure that all planned targets are met within agreed budgets and time scales	Monthly management reports on: • expenses • sales • staffing	For year ending 31 December 2003: Not more than $X million expenses Target is $Y million < 5% increase in costs	Reports due one week after month end
	Budget variance reports	Not more than ± 5%	Reports due one week after month end
Ensure that regional and branch offices comply with operating policies and procedures	Internal audit reports Specific management reports	Agreed standards of compliance As agreed with General Manager from time to time	Quarterly reports agreed with Internal Auditor As agreed
Behavioural criteria	Decisiveness Planning and organising Problem analysis Work standards	Interpersonal sensitivity Management control Initiative	Persuasiveness Leadership Judgment

FIGURE 5.3 COMBINED JOB DESCRIPTION AND PERFORMANCE PLAN

guidance on the behaviours they should be looking for in the individuals they are assessing. Here are some examples of commonly used characteristics and the behaviour descriptions that might be used in assessing the extent to which an individual has what you are looking for.

- *Accountability*. Effectiveness in carrying out organisational and job responsibilities.
- *Communication*. Ability to speak, listen and write effectively in various job roles and settings.
- *Decisiveness*. Readiness to make decisions and judgments and take action.
- *Initiative*. Ability to influence rather than just accept events, and to act independently or without specific instructions within job framework.
- *Judgment*. Ability to reach sound, logical conclusions after consideration of available data and possible courses of action. Makes decisions that are unbiased and rational.
- *Persuasiveness*. Ability to organise and present ideas or facts in ways that influence others to share the point of view expressed.
- *Planning and organising*. Ability to identify and establish appropriate courses of action by which targets can be accomplished by self and others.
- *Problem-solving*. Ability to identify, analyse, generate possible solutions and solve practical problems; and also to accept solutions and innovations suggested by others.

COMPETENCY-BASED METHODS

Competency-based approaches to employee assessment have developed out of the growing use of competency-based approaches in many areas of human resources management, all of which are affected by the continuing lack of consensus over the 'competency' concept. If we accept that competency is 'the set of behaviour patterns that the incumbent needs to bring to a position in order to perform its tasks and functions with competence' (Woodruffe 1990), then it is clear that competency-based approaches to appraisal are concerned less with what employees achieve on the job than with what they have the capability or competency to do. In other words, these methods assess the individual's potential to perform rather than the actual performance.

Competency-based assessment techniques are probably more useful for employee development than for performance assessment. They can be used to determine which areas of skill, knowledge or interest need to be improved for the individual's career to develop. The employee's present job behaviour will contribute information to that analysis, but the assessment is concerned less with present results than with the medium to long-term outlook.

Advocates of competency-based approaches to human resources management believe that competency-based assessment methods have many uses. Boam and Sparrow (1992), for example, argue that they provide a common language system for improving the selection process, the assessment of career potential and the performance review process; for conveying the nature of effective performance; for facilitating self-assessment and development and as a basis for coaching and training; for developing the business culture; for building successful teams; and for identifying the implications for job and organisational design. Phew!

Boyatzis (1982) is usually credited with giving the competency concept its initial popularity. He defines competency as 'an underlying characteristic of a person'. It could be 'a motive, trait, skill, aspect of one's self-image or social role, or a body of knowledge which he or she uses'. Hornby and Thomas (1989) offer a briefer but equally broad definition of competencies as 'the knowledge, skills and qualities of effective managers/leaders'. The difficulty is that such broad definitions seem to touch on virtually any factor that might be relevant to a person's job performance. Jacobs (1989) is more precise in defining a competency as 'an observable skill or ability to complete a managerial task successfully', while Woodruffe (1990) writes about 'behavioural dimensions that affect job performance'.

Critics of the competency concept, such as Randell (1989), dismiss the term as just a trendy name for 'nothing more, nor less, than glorious human skills'. Boyatzis, however, thinks competencies involve more than skills: he draws a distinction between the aspects of a job that need to be performed competently and the attributes a person must bring to the job in order to perform its requirements competently.

Unfortunately, the debate does not end there. Some prefer to put their emphasis on *competence* rather than *competency*. The British National Council of Vocational Qualifications, for example, defines competency as 'the ability to perform work activities to the standard required in performance'. Others suggest that competencies are simply the observable behaviours that separate effective from ineffective performance. The debate will, no doubt, continue.

Analysing competencies

As with any job analysis process, the first step in competency analysis is to describe in quite specific terms what people actually do. The next step is to identify the skills and knowledge that people need in order to perform those tasks to the required standards or levels. There's little difference between this process and the development of job descriptions and person profiles discussed in Chapter 4. Similarly, the methods used for competency analysis include those, already discussed, for use in job analysis: observation, interviews, questionnaires, checklists, diaries, critical incidents, functional analysis, repertory grid and so on.

If competency analysis is similar to job analysis, what distinguishes competency statements from other forms of job description? These features of competencies are significant.

- They describe the core skills that result in effective performance at the level of the individual job.
- They provide a structured way of describing behaviour and this gives the organisation a common language.
- They are the basis for consistent staff selection and development, providing a clear framework and focus for recruitment, assessment, performance review and training.
- They are concerned primarily with future behaviour.

But the preparation of competency statements for individual organisations or jobs can be a very time-consuming and resource-intensive exercise. Feltham (1992) describes a four-level hierarchy of competencies established by a British supermarket chain: a *major competence* (e.g. people management) is made up of twelve *core competences* (e.g. problem analysis) which is demonstrated by *competence* (e.g. monitoring and controlling staff shortages) and measured by *performance criteria* (e.g. plan adequate cover, keep overtime costs within plan and check schedules). If competency-based approaches require such complexity, it is little wonder that they are often seen as the creature of the human resources department and mainly ignored by managers as a tool for people or performance management.

It is possible to develop generic statements of competences which can be applied across an occupation or an organisation. Less time and resources are needed to develop generic statements, but this advantage will be lost if the descriptions are not sufficiently specific to a particular role or occupation. The example on the next page shows that even generic statements must go into considerable analysis and detail. In Britain, the development of Management Competence Standards began with the use of functional analysis techniques to explore and clarify the management role. From this analysis, four *clusters* of personal competence were identified and then broken down into *dimensions* of personal competence.

But this is by no means the end of the analysis and the description of

Management Competences Project

Personal Competence Model

Clusters of personal competence	Dimensions of personal competence
1. Planning to optimise the achievement of results	1.1 Showing concern for excellence 1.2 Setting and prioritising objectives 1.3 Monitoring and responding to actual against planned activities
2. Managing others to optimise results	2.1 Showing sensitivity to the needs of others 2.2 Relating to others 2.3 Obtaining the commitment of others 2.4 Presenting oneself positively to others
3. Managing oneself to optimise results	3.1 Showing self-confidence and personal drive 3.2 Managing personal emotions and stress 3.3 Managing personal learning and development
4. Using intellect to optimise results	4.1 Collecting and organising information 4.2 Identifying and applying concepts 4.3 Making decisions

competency-related behaviours. Take just one example. Dimension 2.2, 'Relating to others', is further divided into eight *associated behaviours*.

1. Give honest and constructive feedback.
2. Encourage others with conflicting views to openly discuss and resolve issues.
3. Actively build relationships with others.

4. Check when not clear how to interpret others' behaviour.
5. State own position openly.
6. Develop networks to access others' strengths.
7. Encourage and stimulate others to make best use of their individual abilities.
8. Help maintain a focus on objectives when working with others.

Analysis becomes even more detailed, time-consuming and job-specific when we seek to define competences for managers. The next example is also drawn from the UK project, where 'Manage information' was identified as one of the manager's four *key roles*. This key role has nine *units*, and the *element* set out in the box below is only one of three for this unit.

Management Competences Project

Occupational Standards for Managers

Key purpose	To achieve the organisation's objectives and continuously improve its performance
Key role	Manage information
Unit	Exchange information to solve problems and make decisions
Element	Lead meetings and group discussions to solve problems and make decisions

Performance criteria	*Range indicators*
• A suitable number of people appropriate to the context and purpose of the meeting are invited to attend.	• Meetings and group discussions led by the manager involve: – discussion of alternatives – group decision-making – consultation.
• The purpose of the meeting is clearly established with other group members at the outset.	• Problems analysed are to do with operations within the manager's line responsibility.
• Information and summaries are presented clearly, at an appropriate time.	• Meetings are informal and usually characterised by the lack of detailed minutes, rules of procedure or standing orders.
• Style of leadership helps group members to contribute fully.	*(continues)*

Performance criteria	Range indicators
• Unhelpful arguments and digressions are effectively discouraged. • Any decisions taken fall within the group's authority. • Decisions are recorded accurately and passed on as necessary to the appropriate people.	• Those present at the meetings/ discussions are other members of the manager's team.

These examples give some idea of the complexity of the competency-based approach. Defining the competency profile for each job or occupational group will be a daunting task for most organisations. However, national frameworks of vocational qualifications—based on some mix of competences or standards—are increasingly common, and may be adapted by organisations to suit their own needs and circumstances. But that is only the first part of the challenge, for competences are intended to describe the main dimensions of effective performance now and in the future. Thus, if competences are used for assessment purposes, it must be recognised that the assessment covers the employee's future potential as well as current performance.

Of course, competency statements can be used for the assessment of current performance but are better used to assess employees' abilities and development needs than the results they achieve. However, using competences to assess only the current situation seems to be a waste of significant amounts of analysis. Competency-based assessment, therefore, is most useful as a developmental tool—a kind of map that guides individuals from where they are at present to where they need to be in the future. But that map will need to change as individual employees make progress through their organisational and job careers.

PROBLEMS OF ERROR IN PERFORMANCE REVIEWS

In this context, *error* refers to something more than the mistakes of fact or interpretation that might be made during the course of a performance review. Psychologists have long been concerned with what they call the problems of *psychometric error*—errors in measurement that occur because of the psychological predisposition or make-up of the assessor—in performance appraisal and other areas of human resources management. Most people are unaware that they are liable to make these errors. But forewarned is forearmed: knowing about psychometric error puts us on guard.

Halo effect

The halo effect is the tendency for ratings and assessments to be influenced by one or two positive attributes of the individual, resulting in an overall favourable assessment that would not necessarily be supported by a careful consideration of all relevant factors. An overall unfavourable assessment resulting from the undue influence of one or two negative factors is sometimes called the *horns effect*.

Central tendency

Many people have a psychological bias against using extremes and avoid both ends of a rating scale in making their assessments. As a result, their ratings are clustered in the middle of the range and there is little differentiation between outstanding and unacceptable performance.

Harshness/leniency

Ratings that are too high or too low in terms of employees' actual performance will produce an inaccurate or skewed distribution of assessments. Apart from the misleading impression this gives, it can lead to problems when the ratings of different groups are compared.

Similarity/dissimilarity

We are inclined to be favourably disposed towards people who are like us. This means that some similarity in the backgrounds, attitudes or experiences of the manager and the employee—quite unrelated to job performance—can lead to a more positive assessment than is warranted. Equally, dissimilarities between managers and employees can produce unjustifiably negative ratings.

First impression/recency

There is a tendency to judge people on the basis of a recent incident or performance that might not be typical of the whole review period, or on the basis of a single factor or impression—for example, what the employee wore for the interview.

Contrast

Managers can sometimes give an employee an unjustifiably high or low rating in contrast to a very low or high rating given to the previous employee assessed. This happens when employees are compared with each other and not with the performance requirements of their jobs.

Bias/prejudice

Problems with bias and prejudice fall into two categories: one is *conscious* or *unconscious* discrimination set off by age, race, sex, cultural origins, appearance, marital status, social position or personal habits; and the other covers personal judgments about an employee that have no relevance to job performance.

Logical error

Logical error occurs when characteristics or factors that appear to be logically related are given similar ratings, even though they are not actually linked. *Stereotyping* is a type of logical error. It happens when it is assumed that a particular characteristic of an employee will lead on to other characteristics: for example, the employee is a woman; women are sensitive; therefore, this employee is sensitive. A similar effect is *implicit personality theory*, where our views of how different characteristics go together lead us to make assumptions based on one factor (e.g. it is a common but questionable assumption that articulate people are emotionally stable) without examining all the other characteristics of the individual.

Insufficient information

This is not strictly a problem of psychometric error, but insufficient, inadequate, incorrect or unrepresentative information can be a problem in itself for performance reviews. It can lead to other error types, such as halo effect and central tendency.

Attributional error

Some research is concerned less with the potential for error in designing and using rating scales, for example, and more with the ways in which managers try to explain good and bad performance. Fletcher (1993b) invites us to try this little exercise as a way to understand the nature of attributional error.

> Think of an incident where you did not perform as well as you would have hoped. Why did this happen? How would you explain it? When you have mulled that over, move on to another incident, this time one where one of your subordinates (or, if you do not have any, a peer) did not perform as well as you hoped. Again, why did this happen? How would you explain it?

Fletcher predicts that we will attribute our own poor performance mainly to situational or circumstantial factors—an *external attribution*. On the other hand, the main cause of poor performance in others will be seen in their individual characteristics—an *internal attribution*. The risk is that managers will attribute an employee's lack of goal achievement to personal deficiencies and pay insufficient attention to other factors.

WHO SHOULD DO THE PERFORMANCE REVIEW?

It is usually thought that performance reviews should be carried out by employees' own managers because they are in the best position to know how their people have been performing. In the interests of fairness and consistency, some organisations require the review to be checked by the manager's manager. And, especially with results-oriented systems, it is common to ask employees to undertake a review of their own performance as preparation for the interview with their manager.

In addition, depending on the purpose of the review and the nature of the organisation, other people might become involved in the review process. This can extend to other managers, 'third party' reviewers (e.g. school inspectors), organisational peers (e.g. other members of a work group or team), direct reports, professional peers (e.g. people outside the organisation but engaged in the same occupation or profession), customers, and other people who might be familiar with the employee's work. These reviewers will see the employee's performance from a different perspective and, if the objective of the review is to help improve or develop the employee's performance, those different views might be valuable. Indeed, as with any assessment process, involving more people and using more techniques will improve both the reliability and the validity of the conclusions. It is seldom practical, however, to involve many people in the performance review process—especially if the employee is expected to play a significant part in the review.

Generally, the employee's immediate manager will have the best knowledge of the employee's work and behaviour and should be in the best position to make the review. However, the manager might not have the skills needed for effective performance planning and review, and close familiarity with the employee means also that the immediate manager is most likely to produce biased ratings. At the same time, the relationship of the manager and the employee should be strengthened if they are involved with each other in the development of performance plans and the subsequent review of performance. Of course, inadequate or unfavourable assessments could have the effect of compromising that relationship.

Increasingly, managers have less direct and less frequent contact with the employees in their work groups and may have less technical expertise on which to base performance assessments. This strengthens the argument for performance planning and review to be a more participative process. At the same time, the growing use of temporary project groups and task forces sets up the dilemma that some employees might not have someone whom they recognise as their immediate manager. Instead, they are managed from project to project by different team leaders.

One solution to this problem is to establish a system in which project team leaders are given responsibility for planning and reviewing the project-related work and performance of employees, but another manager in the organisation has a broader responsibility for each individual's professional and career development—and for ensuring that salary reviews, for example, are actually carried out.

Another approach is to put the onus for information-gathering on the employee. Thus, a manager whose employees are spread over different locations or travel frequently could ask them to determine (as part of performance planning) how they will provide a complete picture of their activities and performance over the review period. Similar approaches can be taken with employees who have technological superiority over their managers.

Self-assessment

No performance review has much point unless it leads to actions or decisions. A review made by a manager without any discussion with the employee might fulfil an administrative need, but will have little impact on the employee's performance or motivation, or on the relationship between manager and employee. Similarly, a review carried out by the employee alone will be of little use unless it is accepted and acted on by others, but it seems unlikely that will happen. Fletcher (1993b) found a self-appraisal scheme in an airline, but reports that its outputs were ignored in all personnel decision-making—a sure sign that it was not taken seriously.

Involving employees in the review process has become increasingly common for two main reasons. First, organisations concerned at the potential for subjectivity and rating errors in personal or performance reviews have tried to combat this by encouraging employees to participate in the review process. Second, it is assumed, probably correctly, that employees will be more committed to the achievement of their performance plans and more likely to accept the results of their performance reviews if they have played a part in drawing them up.

Employees can review their own performance using just about any of the methods already discussed. The major concern here is the possibility of strong leniency error—the risk that employees will be generous in their self-assessments and thus cause disputes and problems of consistency when their assessments are compared with those made by their managers. Research bears out this concern. It shows that employees are capable of being reasonably accurate and objective in assessing their own performance, but does not show that they are particularly willing to do so. In practice, the ratings that employees give themselves tend to be higher than those given by others. However—and this is encouraging—employees are reasonably modest and realistic when they prepare self-reviews for discussion in a performance interview.

In other words, there is value in having employees prepare for the performance discussion by comparing their actual activities and achievements with the targets or priorities they had earlier agreed. Wider-ranging self-assessments carry risks: more than 80 per cent of people consider themselves to be in the top quartile of all performers, and 98 per cent see themselves in the top half. Of course, that's not statistically possible, but it's an argument you don't need to have!

Another point to consider is the extent to which employees will be involved in their performance reviews. To some degree, this will depend on the style of the performance planning and review system; is it to be—in Norman Maier's (1976) terms—based on a *tell and sell, tell and listen,* or *joint problem-solving* approach? In the first case, it might be sufficient to give the employee a copy of the current year's performance plan and a list of topics the manager wants to discuss during the interview, and ask the employee to think about them. For joint problem-solving, the manager and the employee should have much the same information about the employee's past performance and the organisation's future business plans so that they can both prepare for the discussion. As we see in Chapter 6, it is good practice to encourage employees to lead the discussion of their performance, rather than have the manager's view imposed upon them. Self-assessments can be a useful basis for discussing gaps between the perceptions of employees and their managers, but they do not necessarily lead to the closing of the gap between actual and desired performance.

As employees get more involved in the performance planning and review system and regard it more as a joint exercise, it becomes sensible to share the responsibility for initiating and coordinating the process. That will take some of the administrative load off managers, play down the 'boss–subordinate' power relationship that often impedes open communication and increase the likelihood—in the experience of some organisations—that performance planning and review discussions will actually take place.

Peer reviews

There are two types of peer review, but neither is commonly used in the normal course of performance planning and review. First, peer reviews may be used in educational institutions and the medical profession, for example, to assess an individual's suitability for appointment or promotion. But they are used much less frequently for reviewing performance or results on a regular basis. In the second case, members of a work group may be involved in reviewing the performance of others. This might be done by:

- *rating* other employees, using rating scales provided by the employer, on a range of performance or behavioural characteristics;
- *nominating* an 'outstanding' employee, either overall or on specific characteristics;
- *ranking* the members of the work group, either overall or on specific characteristics, in order from 'best' to 'worst'.

Where work is carried out on a group or team basis, peer reviews might be appropriate if the manager is unable to observe work behaviour closely or consistently, and the members of the work group are not in competition with each other. It can also be useful as a team-building process for groups that are reasonably confident in their skills and relationships. However, research suggests that peer reviews are not necessarily accurate or unbiased (Kane & Lawler 1978). And there is a risk that unfavourable reviews will upset the team's cooperation and harmony, especially where there is competition among team members. A comprehensive program of peer reviews would be very time-consuming.

Peer reviews, as outlined here, are different from 360-degree feedback (see pages 106–13).

Review by subordinates

An inevitable conflict arises when we try to encourage greater employee involvement in performance planning and review. The nature of organisational hierarchy puts managers and employees in a superior–subordinate relationship where one party has formal power and the other is expected to be more or less submissive. The manager is also in charge of the rewards system. Some organisations try to balance this power relationship by having employees review the performance and behaviour of their managers, a process usually known as *upward appraisal* or *upward feedback*.

Research suggests that upward feedback does help to improve performance, but its effectiveness seems to depend on who is being appraised and what they do with the feedback information. In one study, poorly or moderately performing bank managers improved their performance over a five-year period following upward feedback (Walker & Smither 1999). Another study found that performance improvement seems to depend on the manager's self-perceptions: managers who had ratings from subordinates that were lower than their self-ratings improved performance following upward feedback, but there was a decrease in performance for those with subordinate ratings higher than their self-ratings (Johnson & Ferstl 1999).

Walker and Smither suggest that improvements in performance are more likely if managers use the feedback to set performance improvement targets and monitor their progress toward those goals. This builds on Locke and Latham (1990), who argue that the goals people set as a result of feedback are the cause of behaviour change, not the feedback itself. This point is discussed in Chapter 4.

Perhaps the main problem with upward feedback is that relatively few managers will be willing to subject themselves to formal appraisal by their subordinates, especially as there is no conclusive evidence that upward reviews generally lead to better performance. Both managers and subordinates may feel threatened by the process and provide responses based on expectations rather than reality.

Of course, there is nothing to stop managers seeking feedback on their management style, and many do so. Managers who have strong and open relationships with their direct reports and other subordinates can ask specific questions about the impact of their management style, and seek suggestions on how they might be more helpful and supportive of their employees. Attitude surveys are used in many organisations to identify particular skills or behaviours that managers should improve or change. And performance review forms might ask employees to give

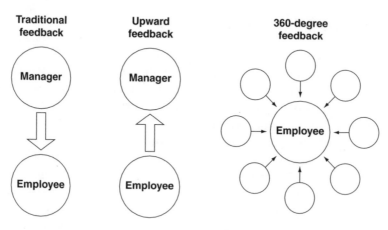

FIGURE 5.4 FEEDBACK METHODS COMPARED

examples of situations in which their managers could have provided more support or resources.

The credibility and effectiveness of an upward appraisal process probably depends primarily on the strength of the relationship—and especially the degree of trust—between employees and their managers. If the relationship is strong there may be no need for a formal upward review, since employees probably communicate their views to managers anyway, but equally no harm would be done if it were included as part of the review process.

360-degree feedback

The use of *360-degree feedback* is becoming more common as organisations seek to produce more complete and rounded assessments. This approach involves seeking the views of all those in the circle surrounding the employee, hence the reference to 360 degrees. Because views are sought from a range of different people, the technique is also known as *multi-rater assessment* or *multi-source feedback*. Whatever name it is given, 360-degree feedback is based on two main ideas.

- Different people have different perspectives, and thus see each other differently. Our relationships with others and our understanding of ourselves will benefit from seeing ourselves as others see us. Edwards and Ewen (1996) say that 'no organisational action has more power for motivating employee behaviour than feedback from credible work associates'. Moreover, 'in the socially-constructed world in which employees work, others' judgments about them (no matter how biased they may be) constitute an important reality' (London & Smither 1995).

- Many employees view the judgments of their co-workers as more fair, accurate and believable than those of their managers, who often have less opportunity to observe the actual work that is done. It is also possible that employees will be more willing to change their behaviour to gain the respect and liking of their colleagues than to win praise from their managers.

In two important respects, 360-degree feedback is different from other assessment methods. First, it is used mainly for assessing managers, not all employees. Second, the focus of 360-degree feedback is almost always 'feedback' for development purposes rather than 'appraisal' or 'review' for assessment. It can be used to assess both *performance* (against previously agreed targets and standards) and *competence* (whether the employee has the skills or behaviours needed for effective job performance), but may be more useful for assessing behaviours, skills and competences and for determining training and development needs and desirable behavioural changes. The evidence is that 360-degree feedback works best when the results are used for developmental feedback, and not for decisions about remuneration or promotion (DeNisi & Kluger 2000). Indeed, there are good reasons for limiting 360-degree feedback to development (Atwater & Waldman 1998).

- Raters may adjust assessments which they think are to be used for performance appraisal, usually making them more favourable. Sometimes, however, a manager sees an opportunity for retribution and reduces a rating.
- 'Game-playing' can occur when ratings are used for appraisal. Managers might try to influence how their direct reports rate their performance, at the expense of meeting organisational goals. They might simply offer a trade: 'You give me a good rating and I'll do the same for you!'

Fear of the consequences of assessing their managers might lead some employees to boycott the 360-degree feedback process. Participation is usually voluntary, but organisations should be very concerned when participation rates are low, or decline.

Determining the objectives. As with any approach to employee assessment, organisations must think about their objectives when contemplating the introduction of 360-degree feedback. There is a long list of possibilities:

- to identify training and development needs
- to improve employee motivation
- to encourage systematic career and personal development
- to promote and develop leadership skills
- to improve skills levels generally
- to provide information for performance planning and review
- to increase self-awareness
- to increase the awareness and understanding of team members
- to clarify the behaviours expected of employees
- to improve communications and working relationships
- to acknowledge the value of all views and opinions.

Implementing the system. Once the objectives have been decided, there is a further series of questions to be asked about how the 360-degree feedback system will be organised and implemented. These questions have been posed (see box below) as a set of choices for United Kingdom government agencies. (Cabinet Office 2001). Generally, where the system's objectives are to improve communication or identify training and development needs, participation tends to be voluntary, the system is part of a wider employee development process, it is more open, and data belongs to the participants (with steps taken to ensure that there is no inappropriate disclosure of individual information).

360-degree feedback: System choices

Anonymous	*v*	Open
Voluntary	*v*	Compulsory
Participant's choice of respondents	*v*	Respondents chosen by organisation
Confidential (data belongs to participant)	*v*	Data belongs to organisation
Results fed back by consultant	*v*	Results fed back by boss
Scored against set standards	*v*	Scored against changes in self over time
Part of wider development process	*v*	Used in isolation

What data is needed for feedback? The indicators that most organisations use for assessing performance—for example, sales volume, production and quality statistics, profitability, return on investment, costs—are not usually the subject of 360-degree feedback. It is more likely to be concerned with *how* people behave than with *what* they do. For example, an organisation that wants its managers to encourage collaboration and team work among its employees will ask the employees specific questions about their managers' leadership style and communications behaviour.

Organisations are also becoming more interested in considering employees' and customers' opinions on such issues as organisational communication, morale, values, decision-making processes, quality and service (Ward 1997). Any of these subjects might be included in 360-degree review processes.

When gathering information, the key is to ask specific questions about specific behaviours—'How often does Person A present you with a clear and up-to-date picture of the team's progress towards its goals for the year?'—and not invite vague and generalised judgments—'Do you find Person A to be an inspiring team leader?' We can take this a step further. If you want information that will help you prepare feedback on, for example, a manager's communicating skills, it would be more useful to focus on the constituent behaviours of that competence—listening, speaking, writing and giving presentations, for example—than to ask for an overall assessment of the manager's 'communicating' abilities.

How is feedback data gathered? Some organisations use trained assessors and facilitators to gather views and data, others use standard-form structured questionnaires and an increasing number use their in-house computer networks. It can be tempting to cast the information net very widely, but there is some evidence that direct reports and next-in-line managers are best placed to provide feedback that actually helps people to develop or improve behaviours that are linked to better executive performance (Sala & Dwight 2002). It seems that next-in-line managers and direct reports have a better vantage point and more direct contact with managers for the activities and responsibilities that are significant for their performance overall.

Feedback data is most commonly gathered by questionnaire. Standard formats can be bought 'off the shelf' and used with or without adaptation, or a series of questions might be developed for the particular organisation or operating unit. Which is better? 'Off-the-shelf' questionnaires:

- are usually prepared by specialists who have the expertise needed to produce reliable and valid instruments
- have usually been subjected to rigorous validation testing
- probably cost less than the time-consuming and expensive process of developing a custom-made questionnaire
- often use industry or occupational norms, so that comparisons can be made with other people in similar situations outside the organisation.

On the other hand, an 'off-the-shelf' questionnaire might not:

- cover all the competency areas that are important for your organisation
- assess the types of competency or styles of behaviour considered desirable for your organisation
- use norm groups that are comparable with your organisation or employees.

Developing a questionnaire. The preparation of a 360-degree feedback questionnaire must begin with a thorough job analysis and a careful determination of the competencies and behaviours appropriate to the particular job role. As we saw in Chapter 4, this is a major exercise, and is even more formidable if the areas for assessment are to be ranked in order of importance or priority.

Some formats use only open questions. This has the advantage of giving assessors unlimited scope for comment but immediately sets up huge problems of data-processing. More commonly, assessors are asked to rate each behaviour on a scale but this can also give rise to problems of information overload.

Take the example of rating a person's ability to communicate. Communicating includes such behaviours as listening, speaking, writing and giving presentations. In more detail, *listening* might include 'using appropriate body language (e.g. nodding)', 'asking questions', 'summarising what is said' and 'letting you finish without interrupting'. In even more specific detail, *appropriate body language* could include 'facing you while you're talking', 'looking you in the eye', 'keeping still', 'leaning forward to show interest', 'nodding' and otherwise signifying agreement with and acknowledgment of what is being said (Ward 1997). It's not difficult to see how a questionnaire could become long and unwieldy.

On the other hand, highly structured questionnaires that limit responses to a tick in a box or the circling of a number may not engage respondents, and can lead to bland and uninteresting feedback.

For that reason, questionnaires usually include space for employees to offer narrative comments.

An example of a 360-degree feedback questionnaire, adapted from a professional services organisation, is given in Figure 5.5.

Name of employee being assessed ....

Is this a self-assessment? ☐ Yes ☐ No

If 'No', you have been nominated by the employee who is being assessed as one of a number of people both inside and outside our organisation who can provide valuable input to this employee on his/her performance. Your individual responses will remain anonymous, and only composite information will be provided to the employee.

To rate how well the person performs in each competency area, please circle a number on the scale, based on these descriptions:

- **(9–10) Shows exceptional skill.** This employee consistently exceeds behaviour and skills expectations in this area.

- **(7–8) Shows strength.** This employee meets most and exceeds some of the behaviour and skills expectations in this area.

- **(5–6) Shows appropriate ability.** The employee meets a majority of the behaviour and skills expectations in this area.

- **(3–4) Development area.** The employee meets some behaviour and skills expectations in this area, but sometimes falls short.

- **(1–2) Needs improvement.** The employee consistently fails to reach behaviour and skills expectations in this area.

- **(N) Not applicable**, or **Not observed**.

Provides best services possible

1. Actively participates and contributes to office teams and team work	N 1 2 3 4 5 6 7 8 9 10
2. Accepts responsibility for all company products and services	N 1 2 3 4 5 6 7 8 9 10
3. Coordinates products and services with other departments, distributors and end customers	N 1 2 3 4 5 6 7 8 9 10
4. Engages in activities which enhance the employee's professional knowledge and skill	N 1 2 3 4 5 6 7 8 9 10
5. Represents the company in a professional manner, both within and outside the office	N 1 2 3 4 5 6 7 8 9 10
6. Recognises and respects the contributions of others	N 1 2 3 4 5 6 7 8 9 10
7. Identifies opportunities for improving operational policies, procedures and techniques within the company	N 1 2 3 4 5 6 7 8 9 10

FIGURE 5.5 360-DEGREE FEEDBACK DATA COLLECTION *(CONTINUES)*

8. Coordinates well with other managers and employees	N	1	2	3	4	5	6	7	8	9	10
9. Effectively communicates company information to customers, suppliers, other managers and employees generally	N	1	2	3	4	5	6	7	8	9	10

Operational skills and proficiency

10. Is proficient in the operation and use of all computer and communications systems	N	1	2	3	4	5	6	7	8	9	10
11. Is proficient in the operation and use of XXX (the company's proprietary service)	N	1	2	3	4	5	6	7	8	9	10
12. Prepares proposals and reports in the prescribed formats; ensures written communications are clear, accurate and timely	N	1	2	3	4	5	6	7	8	9	10
13. Initiates appropriate actions to deal with unexpected events, e.g. updates and provides information about products and services which meet users' requirements	N	1	2	3	4	5	6	7	8	9	10
14. Has a sound understanding of relevant technical and scientific principles	N	1	2	3	4	5	6	7	8	9	10
15. Maintains an appropriate environmental scan and situational awareness.	N	1	2	3	4	5	6	7	8	9	10
16. Uses guidance and professional expertise from elsewhere in the company and outside when appropriate.	N	1	2	3	4	5	6	7	8	9	10
17. Performs on-site system recoveries and can restore network communications when needed	N	1	2	3	4	5	6	7	8	9	10

COMMENTS

Add or attach any written comments on these or any other areas. **Please limit comments to items that concern the individual's performance.**

....
....
....
....
....

FIGURE 5.5   360-DEGREE FEEDBACK DATA COLLECTION

Completed questionnaires (whether on paper or on computer) are usually sent to a central location for processing and preparation of feedback reports. In many cases, to preserve the confidentiality of the people who provided data, processing is done by an external and independent agency.

Providing feedback. Once the questionnaire information has been processed, the results can be fed back to the employee concerned. There are three common feedback methods.

- The employee meets one-to-one with an expert facilitator, usually an external consultant or specially trained internal manager. They discuss the feedback results in detail and the facilitator assists the employee to prepare a development plan.
- A written report is sent directly to the employee. The report summarises the feedback results and might identify areas where change or improvement appears to be needed.
- Where the members of a work team have contributed feedback information about each other, a group feedback session can be held with the assistance of an external facilitator or an internal human resources/management development specialist. The facilitator encourages the members of the group to share and discuss their feedback and to help others to understand the points being made.

Regardless of the method used, feedback is usually focused on the employee's future personal and career development, or the employee's performance in comparison with any performance plans and previous reviews, or a particular behavioural characteristic or competency (e.g. team leadership).

Reviews by outsiders

Some organisations go outside their own walls to seek views and comments on the performance of the organisation and its employees. For example, an organisation's customers might be asked for their opinions of the performance and service received from staff involved with, say, sales, despatch, inquiries and accounts. This can be done by questionnaire or by structured or unstructured interview, conducted by the organisation's own managers or by outside consultants.

TRAINING FOR REVIEWERS

Given how important performance planning and review can be for both organisations and individuals, it is surprising how little attention is given to ensuring that managers and other reviewers have the understanding and skills needed for them to be effective in this activity. Most reviewers would benefit from information or training in several areas.

- *Face-to-face communication skills.* The range of skills and behaviours used in performance discussions is discussed in Chapter 6.

- *Formulating performance targets and standards.* The development of performance standards, indicators, targets and objectives is discussed in Chapter 4.
- *Bias and error in performance reviews.* Reviewers who are aware of the problems of bias and error (see pages 98–101) are more likely to avoid them in their assessments.
- *Observation skills.* Reviewers can be trained to gather data systematically so that it is representative of the employee's full range of behaviours and performance. This adds to the accuracy and acceptability of their assessments.
- *Establishing a frame of reference.* Organisations have different ways of ensuring that terms used in performance reviews—for example, 'effective' and 'ineffective' or 'satisfactory' and 'unsatisfactory'— have the same meaning across several departments or business units. Some incorporate definitions in their review forms (see pages 76–82) or use instruments that include behavioural descriptions (e.g. BARS— see pages 83–5, or BOS—see pages 86–8). Others bring reviewers together to discuss what the expected standards might be and what types of behaviour might be indicative of low, medium or high-level performance. Case studies and role plays can be used to give 'real life' examples.

Of course, the people whose performance is to be reviewed would benefit from some training as well. Effective communication is a two-way process. Some organisations provide employees with one- or two-day workshops designed to acquaint them with the performance planning and review system and give them specific training in communication and related skills. Anything that helps people to deal with the system, and makes them more comfortable and confident in its operation, must enhance performance planning and review.

CHAPTER 6

DISCUSSING PERFORMANCE

The end-of-year interview is often an unpleasant experience for managers and employees, yet it remains the main focus of the performance planning and review process in many organisations. There is no doubt that people who are comfortable with one-to-one communication find the interview less stressful than those who are less confident communicators, but the basic reasons for the unpleasantness of the interview experience lie elsewhere. They are discussed in earlier chapters: the focus here is the communication process itself.

A few organisations persist with the practice of preparing written performance reviews which are then placed on the employee's file. Some tell the employee what the review contains, others don't. Some give the employee an opportunity to comment, others don't. Reviews that are restricted to one-way communication, or no communication at all, are not the subject here. Organisations that don't communicate their performance reviews to employees might be making future legal difficulties for themselves. More important, they should probably ask how a review can be expected to influence the performance or motivation of the employee if its contents are not communicated.

We'll assume that the organisation uses a one-to-one meeting between a manager and an employee as the vehicle for discussing the performance review, and that the employee is given some opportunity, and encouragement, to participate in the review. If we want employees to participate, it might be better to drop the term *interview*, with its connotations of one person asking and the other person answering questions, and call this meeting a performance *discussion*.

As with other aspects of its performance planning and review system, the organisation must first decide on the purpose of the performance discussion. Is it the occasion for managers to tell employees what judgments or appraisals have been made of their performance and contribution, and how they can improve? Or is it an opportunity for managers to share their views with employees and seek their responses? Or does the organisation want to involve employees in the assessment of their performance and incorporate their suggestions as to how that performance might be changed or improved?

Norman Maier (1976) labels these three approaches to appraisal interviewing as *tell and sell*, *tell and listen*, and *problem-solving*. His detailed analysis of each style is presented in Figure 6.1.

	Tell and sell	Tell and listen	Problem-solving
Objectives	• Communicate evaluation • Persuade employee to improve	• Communicate evaluation • Release defensive feelings	• Stimulate growth and development in employee
Psychological assumptions	• Employees desire to correct weaknesses if they know about them • People can improve if they choose to • Superiors are qualified to judge subordinates	• People will change if defensive feelings are removed	• Growth can occur without correcting faults • Discussing job problems leads to improved performance
Role of interviewer	• Judge	• Judge	• Helper
Attitude of interviewer	• People profit from criticism and appreciate help	• One can respect the feelings of others if one understands them	• Discussion develops new ideas and mutual interests
Skills of interviewer	• Persuasiveness • Patience	• Listening and reflecting feelings • Summarising	• Listening and reflecting feelings and ideas • Using exploratory questions • Summarising
Reactions of employee	• Suppresses defensive behaviour • Tries to cover hostility	• Expresses defensive behaviour • Feels accepted	• Problem-solving behaviour
Employee's motivation for change	• Use of positive or negative incentives or both • Extrinsic: motivation is added to the job itself	• Resistance to change reduced • Positive incentive • Extrinsic and some intrinsic motivation	• Increased freedom • Increased responsibility • Intrinsic motivation: interest is inherent in the task

FIGURE 6.1   NORMAN MAIER: THREE APPROACHES TO THE PERFORMANCE DISCUSSION *(CONTINUES)*

Possible gains	• Success most probable when employee respects interviewer	• Employee develops favourable attitude towards superior, which increases probability of success	• Almost assured of improvement in some respect
Risks for interviewer	• Loss of loyalty • Inhibition of independent judgment • Face-saving problems created	• Need for change may not be developed	• Employee may lack ideas • Change may be other than what superior had in mind
Probable results	• Perpetuates existing practices and values	• Permits interviewer to change views in light of employee responses • Some upward communication	• Both learn, because experience and views are pooled • Change is facilitated

FIGURE 6.1   NORMAN MAIER: THREE APPROACHES TO THE PERFORMANCE DISCUSSION

The important point is that the organisation cannot choose a style for the appraisal interview or performance discussion independently of its overall approach to performance planning and review. This meeting is an opportunity to summarise and review performance over a period of time or the duration of an assignment or project, and must be closely connected in both content and style with the whole performance management process. Similarly, a decision about the style of the performance discussion should be made in the context of the organisation's overall management style and approach. Moreover, the type of discussion that is appropriate for the objectives and style of the performance planning and review process will affect the conduct and communication of the discussion itself. What is the nature of the communication? What are the roles of the participants?

As we saw in Chapter 3, inherent conflicts in the performance planning and review process make it likely that managers and employees will have different perceptions of the purpose of the performance discussion, and different goals for their meeting. These differences can interfere with their communication and affect how well they understand the messages they are trying to convey to each other. Look back to Figure 3.1 on page 27 and ask whether it is possible to hold a completely open and honest discussion that meets the organisation's need to develop its employees, and meets employees' needs for feedback, yet protects the employee's self-image and access to rewards.

Maier stresses the importance of deciding on the purpose of the performance discussion. He says that an interview designed 'to let employees know where they stand' suggests that a complete report on performance and other factors will be given, whereas a meeting designed 'to recognise employees for good work' suggests that the content of the interview will be selective and favourable to the employee.

In terms of style, an interview that has the purpose of communicating a review or pay decision will be more *directive*. The manager tells the employee the decision, may give reasons for the decision and explain the process used to reach it, and then listens for a response or looks for a reaction. But the decision itself is not really open to discussion or change. If the employee were encouraged to question the decision, and perhaps try to persuade the manager to change the rating, the manager would be put in a defensive position. Thus, open discussion is ill-advised in 'tell and sell' or 'tell and listen' situations.

On the other hand, openness is essential if the purpose of the discussion is to encourage employees to assess their own behaviour, suggest ideas for change or improvement and commit themselves to specific performance targets. But there must be no suggestion that the manager has already made a decision. An open discussion will, almost by definition, be less structured and the manager will adopt a *non-directive* style.

The relationship between managers and employees is a key factor here. A manager might genuinely want to know what an employee thinks or feels. But if the employee is not accustomed to being asked for an opinion on a day-to-day basis, the responses in the interview are likely to be cautious and, possibly, defensive. Similarly, a manager who relies on control in the workplace—who gives detailed work instructions, requires regular reports and personally checks progress frequently— might find it difficult to encourage cooperation in the performance discussion. The employee will expect to be told what to do. A change of style and behaviour on the part of the manager to encourage the employee to contribute and co-operate might be greeted with suspicion.

It is also important to decide whether remuneration is to be part of the performance review discussion. The case for separating performance reviews and remuneration decisions is argued in Chapter 8. Most organisations combine them, at least in part, but discussion of remuneration, or an expectation that the performance interview is part of the remuneration decision process, might hinder open and frank communication— especially about performance problems or weaknesses. It should be made clear from the outset if remuneration is to be included in the performance review.

PREPARING FOR THE DISCUSSION

The best preparation for the performance discussion is . . . preparation. But busy managers can easily overlook the forthcoming round of performance discussions and leave their preparation to the last minute. This will be obvious to the employees and convey all the wrong signals about the commitment of the manager—and the organisation—to the performance planning and review process. Asking the employee to wait a few minutes while you finish what you're doing, and then searching a cluttered desk for the papers you need will also tell the employee that you don't take this discussion very seriously. Why should the employee take the discussion any more seriously?

Preparation for the performance review should have begun when the manager and the employee agreed on a performance plan. That might have happened a year before. In the meantime, the manager should probably have been keeping a diary of the employee's behaviour and performance, noting both the highlights and the low points, recording any agreed changes in objectives or targets, and jotting down reminders of changes in circumstances that affect the employee's performance. The diary is not part of the review, but it will contain valuable information for the manager's review preparation. Our memories are, at best, imperfect; we are more likely to recall recent events or particular incidents than we are to retain a representative sample of a year's experiences. We need to guard against that potential for bias and error.

We should also make time to review the performance plan made at the beginning of the period or project and consider, in particular:

- the targets agreed when the performance plan was drawn up
- actual achievements, or progress towards achieving targets, since the plan was drawn up
- the reasons why targets have not been achieved, or why there has not been satisfactory progress towards their achievement
- the context in which the employee's performance occurred and any relevant changes in the organisation's situation or circumstances
- any changes that have taken place in the actual job scope or responsibilities of the employee during the period to be reviewed
- the employee's relationships with other staff and, where appropriate, with customers or other people outside the organisation
- any training or development activities undertaken by the employee during the review period.

If planning for the next period's performance is part of the same discussion, the manager will need to think about the job the employee is doing and whether the job description needs to be changed, how the performance of the employee can best contribute to the achievement of the department's goals, and how that might be translated into SMART targets (see pages 56–9) for the employee.

Obviously, effective preparation for the interview will take time and a manager who has to discuss performance with several employees will need to set aside enough time for preparation. This fact underlines how important it is for the organisation, and its managers, to take the process of performance planning and review seriously and to regard it as an essential ingredient in the performance management recipe. Only when managers recognise performance planning and review as an important part of their skills set and organisational responsibilities—and no longer see it as yet another nuisance imposed on them by the human resources department or some other corporate group—will they behave in ways that encourage employees to see performance planning and review in the same light.

Employees should also be encouraged to prepare for the performance review discussion. Their preparation should be similar to that undertaken by managers—a review of the performance plan, any changes in responsibilities or priorities, the reasons why targets have been met or not met, and so on. Employees can probably gather quite a lot of the data needed for the discussion and begin to plan their own future work objectives. This preparation by employees makes it easier for them to play a real and constructive role in the performance review discussion. This is especially relevant in an environment where mutual goal-setting and shared problem-solving are encouraged, but may be less important where the performance appraisal interview is concerned mainly with conveying the manager's judgments of the employee.

Employees should be given written guidelines on how performance is assessed and, if they are to take an effective part in a discussion, should have appropriate training in communication skills, in how to plan and write goals and targets, and in other aspects of the performance planning and review process. Many organisations introduce employees to the performance planning and review system as soon as they join, making it a feature of the induction program and providing employees with detailed information on how the system works. That's an important part of persuading all employees that systematic performance management is 'how we do things around here'.

ARRANGEMENTS FOR THE PERFORMANCE DISCUSSION

Setting an appropriate time and arranging a suitable place for the discussion are obvious first steps.

What is an appropriate time? Both managers and employees have organisational and workload demands that must be met, and getting together a schedule of meetings can be particularly difficult for a manager who has to arrange performance discussions with a number of employees, especially if some of them work in different locations. Employees should be given as much advance notice as possible and asked to prepare for the performance discussion. Some managers find it useful to have a preliminary meeting with employees to agree on the goals of the formal discussion and the major topics they want to cover. This approach helps to get employees thinking about the forthcoming discussion and preparing for it, enabling them to come to the discussion on a more equal basis.

How long will the discussion last? There can be no rule about the 'right' duration for performance discussions. They take time to be effective and produce results, but can lose their effectiveness if they go on for too long at any one time. It's easy to say that a discussion should continue until both manager and employee are satisfied that all the issues have been covered. However, managers don't have limitless time. Equally, many employees are not accustomed to intensive discussions in an office environment and could become bored, distracted or overwhelmed if the discussion lasts too long. It might be necessary to have the review over two or three shorter sessions rather than try to cover all the ground at once.

How many performance reviews can a manager handle? These discussions differ from most meetings that managers have with their employees; they can be tiring and sometimes draining—especially if the news is not all good! Few managers are able to cope with a series of discussions, one after another, over a day or two. That would be too difficult, and employees towards the end of the line would probably not receive the audience they deserve. If all performance review discussions have to be conducted at one time—at the same point in the year rather than spread according to the anniversary of the employee's appointment, for example—managers need to set up a schedule that allows them adequate time between discussions to reflect and prepare for the next meeting, and to carry on with the normal tasks of managing. The schedule of discussions might extend over several days or weeks.

Where is a suitable place to hold the interview? Choice of venue for the performance review needs consideration. There are some obvious requirements. The setting should be private and free from interruptions. Telephone calls and casual visitors should be stopped, and people passing by should not be able to look in on the discussion. It's often suggested that managers should come out from behind their desks and sit with no physical barriers between them and the employees. That advice is generally sound, unless the attempt to make the discussion more comfortable and relaxed has the opposite effect. Some people feel threatened or apprehensive if others get too close. Employees who communicate effectively with their managers across a desk throughout the year might find it difficult to communicate as effectively in a different setting—and that would be particularly ironic if the changed arrangement was intended to make communication easier.

Typically, performance interviews are held in the manager's office. This might be convenient, but it's worth considering a neutral venue—a small meeting room, for example—if that would put the participants on a more equal footing and encourage the employee to engage in a more open discussion. As open-plan workspaces replace more and more partitioned offices, the need for a private and undisturbed meeting place becomes more important. The best advice might be to choose a venue and organise it in such a way that the best possible communication is achieved.

THE STRUCTURE OF THE DISCUSSION

If the purpose is simply to convey the manager's performance review to the employee, the structure of the discussion needs little consideration. The employee will be invited in and asked to be seated; the manager will attempt to get the discussion started with some general non-work conversation; will then tell the employee the substance of the review; perhaps invite comments; then seek to set some objectives for the next year; ask if the employee has any questions or comments; and finally close the discussion. In this scenario the communication is almost entirely one-way, the environment is artificial and uncomfortable, the experience is probably unsatisfactory for both manager and employee—and little will be done to strengthen their relationship and improve or develop the employee's performance.

It will confirm the view held by some that performance appraisal systems are just another form of managerial manipulation. Hartnett (1981), for example, claims that

> stripped of its mystification and mythmaking, performance appraisal functions to maintain managerial control within hierarchically structured, authoritarian organisation. It achieves this function through consolidating judgments about individual performance in the supervisor's hands, by objectifying that judgment through appraisal and rating schemes and thereby conditioning employee behaviour to ensure a favourable assessment.

To reduce these implications of *control* rather than *communication*, organisations and managers should try to ensure that the performance discussion is a genuine two-way process. At the simplest level, the employee must be allowed to do at least half the talking! The discussion is about the employee's performance, not about the manager. In practice, managers commonly do twice as much talking as the employee, though they sincerely believe that participation in the discussion has been equally balanced.

Using questions rather than statements and descriptions rather than judgments will encourage the employee to contribute. Listening carefully, not interrupting, looking for signals in the other person's face and body movements, responding appropriately to any tension, dealing with the employee's questions and comments: these are all skills that will improve two-way communication. They are discussed later in the chapter.

The manager will probably draw up a plan for the discussion, as a way of ensuring that all important points are covered. In outline, that plan—which could be more structured than the interview itself turns out to be—might follow the pattern shown in the box below.

Outline plan for a performance discussion

1. Warm up
This can be the most difficult part of the discussion, because both manager and employee may be apprehensive about what is to come. Talking about something interesting that happened in the workplace recently can ease the tension, but the initial objective is to ensure that the employee understands and accepts the objectives of the meeting and the sequence that it will follow.

2. Job responsibilities
Getting the employee to talk about the job and its current responsibilities and priorities is a way to encourage the employee to start the discussion off. If the interview starts with the manager's views of the employee's job responsibilities or performance, it will inevitably continue in a style that is more directive than participative.
- *What do you see as your major responsibilities at present?*
- *What are the priorities? Why?*
- *What would you change about your job?*
- *How could your time and talents be used better?*

3. Performance goals
Discussing the targets and goals agreed at the last performance review will focus the discussion, which should also explore whether these goals proved to be appropriate and attainable.

- *Overall, how do you feel about the targets we set?*
- *Have any of them proved to be inappropriate? Why?*

4. Job accomplishments

Considering the major achievements of the review period will also help to focus the discussion. It is better for the assessment to be couched in descriptive terms at this stage—judgments may lead to allegations of fault and blame where things have not worked out.

- *How do you feel the job is going?*
- *What has interested you most in your job in the past year?*
- *What have been the major accomplishments?*
- *Where do you think you are being most effective in your job?*

Sometimes it will be better to ask what an employee has been doing rather than what has been accomplished. Like the computer system installation described on page 63, *doing* might prove to be a more positive contribution than *accomplishing*. This is especially true in management positions, where the primary goal is to achieve results through other people. Measuring those results is not a measure of the manager's own performance: what we need to find out is what the manager did to help those other people to achieve the results.

5. Areas for improvement

Again, it is important here to keep the discussion positive and forward-looking: it should focus firmly on how to improve existing performance and overcome any problems or barriers. Trying to establish reasons for past failures will almost certainly lead to discussions of fault and blame, and may force both manager and employee into aggressive or defensive behaviour, which is unhelpful.

- *What disappoints or frustrates you most about your job at the present time?*
- *Where do you feel least effective?*
- *What can we do to help you increase your effectiveness?*
- *What help or support can I give you?*

6. Assessment

Ultimately, the purpose of a performance review is just that. So, however much input there might be from employees, essentially they want to know what the manager—and, by implication, the organisation as a whole—think of their performance and contribution. That assessment should be well balanced. Care must be taken to avoid the errors outlined on page 98–101 and, at the same time, the manager should be thinking about the impact that the assessment might have on the employee. For example, a minor criticism of an otherwise well-performing employee might dominate that individual's understanding of the assessment. Similarly, the manager who treads warily and chooses words carefully in order not to upset a poor performer might leave that employee with the impression that things are rather better than is actually the case.

7. Plans for improvement

The manager will have some ideas of areas of performance or behaviour which can be improved, and should think about possible solutions. These should not be imposed, but discussed and agreed with the employee. If possible, the employee should be encouraged to lead the discussion of possible improvements. Building on the employee's ideas is more positive than having the employee respond to the manager's ideas. Their subsequent agreement on action will then give a positive platform for future discussions and performance.

8. Conclusion

Ending a performance discussion can prove more difficult than many would anticipate. Preparing to close, once the discussion has ended, is as important as preparing the opening. Summarise the discussion; agree on future action, including anything the manager has undertaken to do; describe what will happen with the results of the review; thank the employee for their time and contribution to the discussion; and end the meeting.

To conclude this examination of the structure and contents of the performance discussion, here are some key points for consideration.

- **Preparation and participation.** Both managers and employees need the communication skills and techniques discussed in the next section. Similarly, both must prepare for the performance discussion and they must participate actively.
- **Relevance.** The performance discussion should focus on matters that are relevant to the individual's job or employment. If there are personal issues to be discussed, make time for a separate meeting outside the performance planning and review framework.
- **Discipline.** Disciplinary action is not part of performance planning and review. Performance that is 'below standard' or 'unacceptable' might be the subject of criticism during the discussion, but any

disciplinary action or steps towards termination of employment should be taken separately. In his final letter to General Electric's stockholders, the outgoing Jack Welch commented that companies must love and nurture the top 20 per cent of their employees, and actively weed out the bottom 20 per cent. Performance appraisal was his preferred weapon for that task. Nothing will compromise a performance planning and review system faster than an impression among staff that it is simply an instrument of discipline or punishment.

- **Using forms.** If the organisation uses performance planning and review forms, they should be available during the discussion so that points can be summarised and agreed actions noted. But completing the form should not be central to the planning and review of performance. Many organisations are abandoning complex and sophisticated forms in favour of formats with plenty of space for the manager and the employee to record the key points of their discussion. If there is a form, it should be openly available to the employee who should be able to comment on any aspects of the review where there is disagreement. Most important, a review form should accurately describe the employee's performance, in terms of the job's responsibilities and any previously agreed standards or targets, so that it is reliable as both a guide and a record.

COMMUNICATION SKILLS

Managers and employees need the same communication skills and techniques for performance planning and review that they need for effective communication generally. But it is still useful to look at communication in the specific context of the performance planning and review discussion. Most effective communication is a two-way process, and this is especially important in a performance discussion that seeks to get the employee's ideas and commitment as much as it serves to tell employees what the manager thinks of their performance. Thus, for both manager and employee, *listening* and *providing feedback* are just as important as *speaking clearly* and *asking questions*. The objective of all communication should be to ensure that there is an effective exchange of understanding.

Asking questions

There are two main types of questions.

- *Open* questions are designed to open up a conversation up and get people talking.

- *Closed* questions are used to summarise or confirm what the other person is saying.

Open questions. These usually begin with one of the common interrogatives—*What? How? Why? Who? When?*—but that doesn't mean the discussion has to become an interrogation. Blunt questions can be softened if they start with phrases like 'Think about . . .' and 'Tell me about . . .', yet retain their essential role as questions that 'open up' respondents and get them talking. The key to open questions is that the other person can only respond sensibly by providing some information: you cannot respond *Yes* or *No* to an open question.

- *How do you think things have been going during the year?*
- *What are you especially pleased about with your performance?*
- *Why do you say that?*

Closed questions. If open questions are opening questions, then closed questions are closing questions. They can usually be answered *Yes* or *No* or by providing a specific piece of information. They are best used to summarise what the other person has said, to check your understanding of it or to close off part of a discussion so you can move on. However, too many closed questions will stifle responses and turn the discussion into an interrogation.

- *Can I help you?*
- *Do you want to give that some more thought?*
- *Is there a better way to do it?*

Each of these questions is easily converted into an open question:

- *How can I help you?*
- *What other thoughts do you have about this situation?*
- *What would be a better way to do it?*

STAR interviews

Getting employees talking should be an early objective in the performance discussion. The STAR approach is designed to encourage employees to talk specifically about their jobs and their performance.

Describe a **S**ituation *that you were involved in where . . .*
Tell me what **T**asks *had to be accomplished.*
What **A**ction *did you take?*
What were the **R**esults?

Probing questions. These are hybrid questions, neither completely open nor completely closed. We use them to get a person to talk in more detail about a topic or event, but they shouldn't be used so frequently that the questioning becomes an interrogation.

- *Could you tell me some more about . . . ?*
- *What do you mean when you say . . . ?*
- *What effect has that had on . . . ?*

The easiest probing question is the one that begins with 'Why' but frequent use of this little word can become a barrage for the listener; just reflect on every parent's experience of children who constantly ask 'why' or 'why not'.

Asking for comparisons—'What do you feel are the advantages and disadvantages of . . .'—is a form of probing question that gets people to explore in more depth the points they are making. Many of us get carried away with our own enthusiasm and start to generalise or exaggerate. We need to be asked to be more specific but may react negatively to a simple denial or disagreement.

Hypothetical questions, starting with queries like 'What would you do if . . . ?', are another technique for getting employees to think about new ideas or possible actions. But they should not be used as a device to avoid talking about real issues. Similarly, people should be discouraged from translating real problems into hypothetical situations: the translation is seldom complete or completely accurate.

Common mistakes with questions. We make three common mistakes when asking questions.

1. *We ask more than one question at a time.* This can leave the other person confused about what we really want to know or which question to answer first. Or the other person may avoid answering any of the questions.
2. *Our questions suggest the answers we want.* This might encourage the other person to choose one of the responses implied in the question, rather than provide the real answer.
3. *We go on talking after we've asked a question.* The other person can't respond, and we can't listen to a response if we're still talking!

Listening

A discussion between two or more people might be a situation where one person is talking and the others are listening. In many cases, however, one person will be talking and the others will be preparing to talk! The loudest signal that people are not listening is 'Yes, but . . .' People who are listening actively don't interrupt or try to impose their views, but prefer to build on what others are saying. However, many meetings and discussions become a succession of statements made by individuals without much attention being paid to what others are saying.

Listening—because it appears to be a passive activity—is a difficult skill to teach or to learn. Yet we must learn to listen actively: to concentrate on what is being said; to assess and try to understand what is said, and what is not said; to stay neutral in this process; and to avoid rushing to quick judgments or making assumptions. And it is not just listening to what people say that is important; we should also listen to how they speak. Does the tone of voice reflect enthusiasm or surprise or anger? Does the person sound confident or nervous on this topic?

Using pauses is a key aspect of listening. In any discussion, a person who keeps on talking neither encourages nor obliges the other person to respond. In a *tell and sell* or *tell and listen* discussion, the employee might be defensive in the face of criticism and simply withdraw. Then, to avoid an awkward silence, the manager goes on talking and the employee has no need to respond or take any further part in what rapidly becomes an uncomfortable, one-way lecture. Pauses—which can go as far as a physical comfort break, or time out to get a drink or have lunch—allow employees to think about ideas or suggestions without the time pressure that often seems to intrude on the one-on-one discussion. Breaks are also an opportunity for participants to gather their thoughts, and can help to relieve any build-up in tension in the interview.

Much has been said and written about *body language*—the notion that what we do with our bodies can convey powerful messages. The listening process involves looking for visual cues about what the other person is thinking or feeling. Has the person who stares out of the window lost interest in the discussion? Does the crossed-arms posture indicate that the employee is on the defensive? Is the person who yawns bored or tired? Are you distracted by someone who is fiddling with a pen?

Paraphrasing and summarising

For many managers and their employees, a discussion that lasts an hour or more will be the longest time they spend in concentrated one-to-one communication in a whole year. It is, for everyone, a long time over which to maintain concentration. *Paraphrasing* what the other person is saying ('What you seem to be saying is . . .') and *summarising* the discussion from time to time ('What I think we've talked about and seem to be agreed on is . . .') have the dual effect of checking that people have the same understanding of what they are discussing, and breaking the discussion up into a series of smaller and more manageable communication steps.

Feedback

Providing feedback to employees is a major objective of the performance review. Lansbury and Prideaux (1981) note that

> feedback is an important part of the learning process. Without it, employees have only their own estimation of how well they are performing and this may be quite inaccurate. Feedback from others can confirm and encourage employees in a mode of behaviour which meets acceptable standards or, alternatively, alert them to the need to change their behaviour.

Like any effective communication, constructive feedback needs to be planned. Perhaps most important, the manager needs personal knowledge—from observation or investigation—of the behaviour or performance that needs change or improvement. Relying on second-hand reports or the rumour mill is not good enough. Next, some people find it helpful to rehearse what they're going to say in these potentially tricky communication situations—not to the extent of writing out and learning a prepared script, but taking a little time to think about and practise what they want to say, how, and in what sequence. Those careful communicators will also think about how the other person will react to what is going to be said and prepare to respond.

Unfortunately, too much feedback in performance discussions is critical and negative. The challenge is to keep a balance between criticism and praise, and this is more likely if you've identified some points of positive feedback in advance. Mention them first, and the employee will realise that you are concerned with the total picture: subsequent criticisms will be seen in that context. It might be a cultural thing for some societies, but many people are not very good at giving or receiving praise. Yet most people respond positively to sincere appreciation of their efforts and a quiet 'thank you' or 'well done' will help to build a positive relationship in which constructive criticism is part of the nurturing process.

Effective feedback is:
- specific rather than general
- descriptive rather than evaluative
- focused on behaviour that can be changed
- concerned with the 'what' of behaviour, not the 'why'
- substantively based so the receiver can check its validity
- timely and relevant to the issues under discussion.

Managers should use real examples of employees' behaviour and describe the effect they have on performance and on the behaviour of others.

Generalisations and judgments—'You're always late' or 'You're not really committed', for example—should be avoided. They lead to argument and resentment. It's much more constructive to say 'You've been late three times in the last two weeks. That means others have to pick up your share of the work until you get here. Is there anything wrong?'

In addition to providing feedback to employees, the performance discussion should be an opportunity for managers to seek feedback from their employees. 'What further advice or support could I provide for you on this project?' 'How do you feel about how well we communicate?' 'Do you feel you have enough information about what is happening elsewhere in the department?'

However, a manager or anyone else who solicits feedback must be ready to deal with it. Any signs of defensiveness—for example, interrupting to justify what the manager did or to blame others—will indicate that the manager doesn't really want to hear the employee's views. It would be better for the manager to paraphrase what is being said without evaluating it, ask for clarification if necessary and summarise the discussion from time to time.

Criticising

Managers might intend to be constructive when criticising employees' performance, but the impact is usually negative. Criticism can encourage employees into defensive behaviour during the discussion, leading them to blame other people and other factors for their own shortcomings. In this way, they can evade responsibility for their own performance and avoid discussing how it might be changed or improved. Moreover, a constant stream of criticisms will have a negative effect on the motivation of employees, who will go away from the discussion with feelings of failure and resentment rather than achievement and encouragement. Subsequently, research shows, their performance will improve least in those areas where they were criticised most.

If employees feel that everyone in the organisation gets criticised during performance review discussions, they will not take criticism of themselves as individuals very seriously. In addition, it is not hard to imagine the negative effect on the performance management process overall if the emphasis appears to be on criticism, constructive or not.

None of this is to say that we should ignore areas of performance where employees fail to meet standards or achieve targets. However, it is more effective to adopt a problem-solving approach to identify the issues and discuss them openly, without concern for fault and blame. Helping people to learn from their mistakes may be hard for some managers but it is a key to successful coaching and effective performance development.

Arguing

Some managers feel that they must argue with their employees over every point of difference or disagreement. Instead, they should understand that attentive listening implies neither agreement nor disagreement, but simply allows employees to say what they want to say. From what they hear, managers can distil the issues that need clarification, verification or action. Arguing points of detail puts both managers and employees into aggressive/defensive roles and hinders the openness of the communication between them.

Counselling

Counselling is an inevitable part of the review process. But the nature of the helpful communication it involves will vary significantly according to the situation and needs of the person being counselled. For managers, the skill or art of listening may be their most important counselling tool; many people simply need to talk to someone about their problems.

Managers' responses will be either *directive* or *non-directive* in style. In the first case, the manager will seek to *direct* the employee's behaviour in a particular direction. This is characteristic of the *tell and sell* or *tell and listen* approach. On the other hand, the *problem-solving* approach will feature *non-directive* counselling in which managers aim to help people solve their own problems by identifying and analysing a range of possible solutions or actions.

Managers need to accept that many problem situations—family problems, alcohol or drug dependency, psychiatric illness, for example—need specialist assistance or treatment. The manager should try to recognise the signals of these situations and help the employee to make contact with professional or expert advisers.

Note-taking

For some people, taking notes during the interview is part of the process of active listening. It shows that they are interested in what is being said and consider it sufficiently significant to be recorded; it helps them to keep focused and maintain the structure and sequence of the discussion. For others, note-taking is a distraction. They find it hard to talk if another person appears to be writing down what they are saying, and are concerned that an ill-formed idea might be quoted against them at a later date. Ultimately, the interaction is physically disrupted if one person is so intent on recording the conversation that the other can see only the top of the note-taker's head!

Notes should be made during the performance discussion. Our memories are not very good. When it comes to setting targets, for example, it's better to have written down what was agreed at the time of planning performance than to argue during the performance review about what was actually intended. Noting down other people's ideas is also a strong signal that they are being taken seriously and will be considered further.

Some managers have developed the skill of getting employees to do the writing during the performance discussion. 'So, how can we express that target?' the manager asks and, as the employee starts to suggest the words, the manager passes across the performance planning form and says 'Sounds good. Why don't you write that down?' The target is then clearly the employee's goal: the act of writing it down adds to ownership and commitment.

Describing performance

Performance reviewers often find it difficult to express how well an employee is performing. Descriptions like 'good interpersonal skills' or 'team player' might give an employee a warm feeling, but they are judgmental rather than informative or developmental. They give the employee nothing to build on. Worse, negative descriptions—'needs to improve interpersonal skills' or 'not a good team player', for example—are useless without specific examples to justify the manager's opinion and indicate where the employee needs to make improvements.

Similarly, during a performance planning discussion, managers must encourage employees to commit themselves to SMART targets and specific actions: it's hard to follow up on an employee's promise that 'I'll try harder'!

A MODEL FORMAT

The performance planning and review forms set out in the following pages are not a model in the sense that they are in some way ideal. Each organisation must design a system, including forms, to suit its own needs and circumstances. However, this model format incorporates many of the points made in this book and it might be helpful to see them laid out in this way.

There are, in fact, two forms: one that can be used for all employees (pages 134–41), and a second—the supplement for managers (pages 142 –3)—which can be added for those who have responsibilities for managing and developing people.

The forms are designed to provide participants with a record of their agreed performance plans and the results subsequently achieved. However, the forms should not be the main focus: the purpose of the performance discussion is to help managers and employees get a better understanding of the contributions that might realistically be expected and a more specific assessment of the employee's actual performance.

In summary, this approach is designed to be forward-looking rather than appraisal-oriented. It is focused on job requirements and job performance, and based on explicit statements of the contributions the employee plans to make. In process terms, this approach is designed to help managers and employees to share the planning and assessment of performance and to encourage more open and regular communication.

This model begins with an explanatory booklet (pages 134–7) which is designed to introduce the performance planning and review system to managers and employees. The forms referred to in the booklet are set out on the following pages.

ABCorporation Ltd

Introducing performance planning and review
Performance planning and review is designed to:
- help staff at all levels and in all parts of ABCorporation by linking performance assessments to specific statements of each person's planned contributions
- help clarify job responsibilities and priorities, and thus help to improve individual and organisational performance
- focus on what each person should contribute to the achievement of the work group's objectives, and in that way help to foster team work.

The elements of performance planning and review
1. The performance plan
2. Interim performance reviews
3. The performance review and summary
4. The management review

How the process of performance planning and review works

1. Based on the overall goals of the organisation, managers outline to staff the objectives and priorities of their departments and work groups for the coming year.

2. Staff members then draft individual performance plans for the year ahead, linking them to the department's objectives and to the main areas of responsibility of their jobs. Staff members also describe the contributions they have made during the previous year.

3. Each staff member then meets with his or her manager to review the previous year's performance and to agree on the performance plan for the coming year.

4. Subsequently, managers discuss the performance plans and reviews of their staff with the next-in-line manager. This ensures consistency in both planning and review and is a safeguard against any possibility of unfairness in the planning and review process.

5. *Interim reviews.* When it is not appropriate to plan for a period of a whole year, or if the requirements of the position change significantly during the year, then the staff member and the manager should meet for an interim review of the performance to date and to agree on any changes that may be needed in the performance plan.

The performance plan

Performance planning and review begins with the performance plan, which is a statement of the staff member's main areas of responsibility and of the contributions expected in each of those areas during the coming year. More specific and personalised than job descriptions, the statements of planned contributions relate the results and standards of performance expected of each staff member directly to the objectives of the work group, the department and the organisation.

The performance plans for managers have a supplement that focuses on their responsibilities for managing and developing people. The statements of planned contributions should:

- focus on expected results and standards of performance and not merely describe activities to be performed
- be specific enough to determine whether they have been achieved
- be clear and understandable to both the staff member and the manager
- be at a level of performance and achievement appropriate to the staff member's position and responsibilities
- mention additional resources, training, experience or management support needed to achieve the contribution.

Interim performance reviews

Interim performance reviews are a discussion of progress towards the contributions set out in the performance plan. They are held as needed, thus providing managers and staff members with an opportunity to modify their performance plans in the light of changing circumstances, particularly those that are outside the staff member's control.

In addition, interim reviews give staff members a chance to request further guidance or information, or other support they may need.

These reviews are more than the normal day-by-day workplace communication and entail more than informal coaching. They are intended to be brief, explicit reviews of the staff member's responsibilities and contributions in relation to the department's work program. The interim reviews should avoid the possibility of surprises and misunderstandings at the time of the year-end review.

The performance review

The performance review focuses on actual contributions in each area of responsibility, rather than simply describing the staff member's activities during the year. It gives both the staff member and the manager the opportunity to discuss performance in terms of their agreed performance plan and to record what results were achieved and how well. Performance reviews should:

- be mainly descriptive
- relate directly to the statements of planned contributions
- be clear and open to encourage staff members to maintain or improve performance and to give managers sound information on which to assess the performance of individuals and the organisation.

The performance summary

The performance summary is designed as a more general and evaluative statement of major performance issues and of recommendations for follow-up action.

The summary of major performance strengths and suggested improvements is designed to help the staff member and the manager to clarify where there is a need for changes in attitude or behaviour, and to assess whether the staff member has any immediate needs for training related to the present job.

Performance reviews and summaries for the previous twelve months are discussed and completed at the same time as performance plans for the coming year.

The management review

The management review meeting has several important functions. It provides senior managers with an overview of the people for whom they have responsibility and, at the same time, ensures that their performance plans and reviews are treated equitably in comparison with others.

It is also an opportunity for the comments of staff members to be taken into account and acted on where appropriate.

The discussion with the more senior manager provides managers with an opportunity to check their assessments of people's performance and the consistency of their plans and objectives with those of the wider organisation. The discussion also gives the more senior manager an understanding of the mix of skills and abilities in each section and how these might develop for the good of the staff and ABCorporation.

The supplement for managers

All staff of ABCorporation, including managers at all levels, are expected to take part in the performance planning and review process. For managers, the technical and business aspects of their positions are covered in the normal performance plan and review.

In addition, there is a supplement for managers, dealing with that most important of their responsibilities: the management and development of the people for whom they have responsibility.

The supplement is designed to focus both planning and review on key management roles such as priority-setting, decision-making, communications, coaching and staff development, delegation and team work.

The supplement recognises that the management and development of people are significant but often overlooked roles for managers.

ABCorporation

Performance planning and review

Name:

Position:

Section:

Plan period
From: To:

Performance plan

The staff member and the manager should develop this plan jointly, normally twelve months before the performance review.

| Name: | Date initiated: | Interim review date: |

Major areas of responsibility	**Planned contributions to section's objectives** What results or standards are expected in each area of responsibility? Describe the agreed actions. Where appropriate, indicate action priorities and target dates.
Changes in plan	May be recorded at any time during the plan period

Optional additional plans Where considered appropriate by the manager and the staff member.

Performance review

Contributions to section's objectives
Before the discussion with the
manager, the staff member describes
what has actually been achieved.

The manager comments

Far exceeded	Consistently exceeded	Exceeded at times	Consistently met standard	Did not meet standard

Additional accomplishments

Performance summary

Overall performance summary
Considering all the factors, summarise the staff member's overall performance during the plan period.
Also note any significant influence on the performance of others.

Major performance strengths

Suggested improvements

What specific training would help improve the staff member's performance?

Performance improvement is needed to meet job requirements:
❐ No   ❐ Yes, in area(s) noted above.

_____

Manager's signature   Name and title

_____   _____   _____

Date discussed   Staff member's signature—to indicate this   Date
with staff member   review has been read and discussed with the manager

Staff member's comments Optional

_____

Staff member's signature—if comments are made   Date

Management review
The reviewing manager should give particular attention to any significant disagreements between the
staff management and the manager, and to plans for action and follow-up on this review.

_____

Reviewing manager's signature   Name and title   Date

Distribution: Original to manager, copy to staff member

ABCorporation

Performance planning and review

Supplement for managers

Managerial responsibilities

The main areas of managerial responsibility are

- managing work programs and budgets
- managing relations with clients within and outside the corporation
- managing relations with others inside the corporation services
- providing technical and policy guidance to ensure desired results are achieved
- managing and developing people.

The first four areas of managerial responsibility should be covered in the performance plan and review. Managing and developing people should be covered in this supplement. The responsibilities listed overleaf may be used to focus attention on those areas of people management where potential benefits are greatest. Where appropriate, note the expected results or standards under each heading.

Managing and developing people

Name: Title   Date initiated:

Planned contribution	Actual contribution	Reviewing manager's assessment
The results or standards expected in each of the areas listed.	To be completed by the manager being appraised.	of extent to which job requirements were met

The assessment columns (rotated labels): Far exceeded | Consistently exceeded | Exceeded at times | Consistently met standard | Did not meet standard

Planned contribution		Far exceeded	Consistently exceeded	Exceeded at times	Consistently met standard	Did not meet standard
Setting priorities and taking decisions						
Communicating clear performance expectations and performance feedback						
Providing guidance and support to staff on their personal development						
Delegating responsibility and encouraging innovation						
Fostering co-operation and teamwork within and between sections						
Other						

Signature of manager making appraisal   Date

Signature of manager being appraised   Date

Signature of reviewing manager   Date

CHAPTER 7

DEVELOPING PERFORMANCE

Any system of performance management inevitably focuses on the process of performance planning and review. These are the activities that demand the time and attention of managers and employees and where organisations develop specific procedures and provide special training. Yet, as we have said earlier, what happens in the relatively long gaps between performance discussions is more important to successful performance management than how well we conduct those discussions or complete the accompanying forms.

Unfortunately, the development of employees' performance is often the forgotten aspect of performance management. Perhaps it's because, unlike performance planning and review, there are no procedural requirements or pressures from top management or the human resources department to get reports in by a set date.

But surely there is little point in setting performance targets if employees lack the skills or knowledge to achieve those goals? Similarly, it's hardly helpful to accept that a lack of skills or knowledge is the reason for poor performance without deciding how the employee is going to acquire those competencies for use in the future. Vague promises about sending people on courses are not what performance development involves. At the same time, a need for training is frequently used as an excuse for poor performance. Managers must be able to identify and handle performance problems without always seeing training as both the problem and the solution. They must also understand that performance has to be managed and developed on the job: instances of inadequate performance cannot be left to a once-a-year review but must be dealt with as they occur.

At a wider level, most organisations now recognise the need for continuing review and renewal so that they can respond to new challenges in their environments. In other words, the concept of the *learning organisation* is now well accepted. For organisations aspiring to that status, the continuing development of performance might be the key factor in the performance management cycle.

The development aspects of performance management are a challenge for most organisations. In the United States, according to a survey taken in 2000, only one in three organisations is satisfied with its development planning (34 per cent of the respondents), 360-degree feedback (33 per cent), coaching (33 per cent) or leadership development (38 per cent). Yet 61 per cent of those organisations were satisfied with their performance management systems overall (SHRM/PDI 2000).

THE MANAGER'S ROLE

Tom Peters has said we no longer need managers who are cops, referees, devil's advocates, dispassionate analysts, naysayers or pronouncers. Instead, we need leaders who are enthusiasts, cheerleaders, nurturers of champions, coaches and facilitators. The differences between managers and leaders are much talked about as organisations try to swap the traditional control model of management for one based on cooperation, and to turn concepts like employee empowerment and self-managing teams into practical reality. But it's not a question of leaders *or* managers: organisations need both.

As Kotter (1990) tells us, successful organisations need good managers to control complexity and effective leaders to produce worthwhile change. Leaders have to set the organisation's direction and motivate people to support it, while managers plan, solve problems, organise and control activities. To manage and develop people and their performance successfully, organisations need both managers and leaders. And you can't separate them. Warren Bennis (1984) describes leadership's contribution in terms that sound like good advice for managers.

> Leadership can be felt throughout an organisation. It gives pace and energy to the work and empowers the workforce. Empowerment is the collective effect of leadership. In organisations with effective leaders, empowerment is most evident in four themes—people feel significant, learning and competence matter, people are part of a community, and work is exciting.

That advice is confirmed by the Gallup Organisation's research on management. It found that 'great' managers don't have much in common, except that they do four things extraordinarily well (Buckingham & Coffman 1999):

- They *select people for their talent*, not simply for their experience, intelligence or determination.
- They *set expectations in terms of the right outcomes*, not the right steps.
- They *motivate people by concentrating on their strengths* rather than identifying their weaknesses.

- They *develop people by helping them find the right fit*, not just pushing them up to the next rung on the organisational ladder.

Traditionally, many managers have relied on formal authority—their *positional power*—to get employees to comply with work instructions and job requirements. The use of authority in this way might get the work done, but it hardly amounts to effective leadership. And it is less and less likely to work with many of our 'new' employees. However, if employees carry out the work willingly and find it rewarding, then we can say that the manager has *personal power* in additional to positional power, and has exercised effective leadership.

In most situations, the successful use of both personal and positional power—based on the approaches to job design described in Chapter 3 and the activities described by Bennis and Gallup—will require managers to use *problem-solving* rather than *tell and sell* as their preferred style of performance management. We should remember, however, that the manager's positional power or formal authority usually includes being able to control rewards and punishment. This has obvious implications for the performance management process and for the relationships of managers/leaders and employees/followers. We're back to the classic dilemma of the manager as both judge and helper.

There is a further issue. As shown in the box below, a manager's power has several different bases and will influence different employees in different ways according to its source. For example, professional and knowledge workers will usually recognise and respect expert and referent power; they may be influenced by information and connection power, they may be cynical about a manager's legitimate power, and will probably reject any overt attempts to use coercive or reward power. But new employees, or those at the lower levels of the organisation, are likely to respond quickly and without question to what they perceive as the legitimate power of a top executive.

Sources of a manager's power

Coercive power is based on fear. People comply because failing to comply leads to punishment.
Legitimate power derives from a manager's position. Subordinates believe managers have the right, because of their positions, to expect compliance with instructions or suggestions. Increases as managers move higher in the organisation.
Expert power flows from a manager's expertise, skills and knowledge,

which are respected by others and thus influence their attitudes and behaviour.

Reward power is a manager's ability to provide tangible or intangible rewards for other people who believe they will be rewarded if they comply with the manager's wishes.

Referent power is based on a manager's personal traits. We are influenced by people we like, admire or identify with.

French and Raven (1959)

Information power derives from the fact that a manager has, or can get, information that others consider valuable.

Connection power is based on a manager's links with influential and important people inside and outside the organisation.

Raven and Kruglanski (1975)

How managers use power, whatever its source, is a significant factor in performance management. We cannot escape the reality that organisations are power systems in which individuals balance their desire for various tangible or intangible rewards against the need to comply with authority in its various forms. McClelland (1970) points out that power can have both a positive and a negative face. *Negative power* is expressed in terms of dominance and submission, where one person exercises power over another who is put at a disadvantage as a result. *Positive power*, on the other hand, is exercised for, or on behalf of, other people. Managers who work with their staff to formulate plans, to decide goals and develop their skills and abilities are using power positively for both the individuals and the organisation.

So how can managers use power positively in managing and developing the performance of their employees?

TRAINING AND LEARNING

Developing people and their performance is not a matter of sending employees off to training courses. Indeed, the most effective training and development is probably done on the job, on a one-to-one basis between managers and employees. In this situation, the manager is a coach, not a trainer. And the employee is learning, not being taught. That might seem rather trite and obvious, but it's worth setting out how we know that this is a more effective approach to performance development, especially for adults.

The main focus of on-the-job coaching and learning is performance development. Learning for its own sake, or learning for personal or career development, are different objectives. Where the aim is to develop an employee's performance, the emphasis must be on ensuring that the person gains and retains the skills and knowledge needed for effective job performance, and is able and willing to apply them. This is not learning for learning's sake, but learning which encourages and equips employees to make desirable changes to their work behaviour.

We go through four stages of learning before changes in behaviour occur. First, we come to *know about* something that is new or different. That knowledge is not useful in itself until the second stage of *understanding* when we recognise the possible applications for the new idea or information. The third stage of *acceptance* is reached when a person has enough knowledge, and understands it well enough, to see the new behaviour as a desirable option. This can be the most difficult stage in learning if it requires us to change our existing attitudes, beliefs or values. We will need to be persuaded of the advantages of making those changes. Finally, we reach the stage of being able to *apply* the new learning: we can recognise where it is applicable, accept the advantages and are willing to make the changes. This final stage is not complete, however, until the new learning has actually been applied and we can see the benefits of the new behaviour.

Few off-the-job training courses are set up to take people through all these stages. In most cases, especially in educational institutions, formal courses cannot go much past the first stage. The use of case studies and experiential exercises might help take the learning into the second and third stages, but the fourth—and most critical—phase can only happen on the job. And it can only happen with the support and guidance of a manager, or some other person playing the role of coach. Learning that leads to performance improvement and development can most effectively be carried out on the job—for a number of reasons.

People learn because they want to

Motivation is a key factor in learning. People who want to learn usually do better than others, which is one reason why mature students frequently achieve better results in higher education courses than younger students. However, we have to know what we want to learn, and why.

Employees who are encouraged to understand how their proposed learning will contribute to achievement of their performance targets should be more enthusiastic about the learning process. That understanding can come from performance planning and review sessions with their managers, or from specific discussions of their performance development needs.

A person's desire to learn is also increased if we provide *intrinsic motivation*—making the job itself or the training more interesting and rewarding—or *extrinsic motivation* in the form of rewards that come as a result of the learning experience. Extrinsic rewards include pay and fringe benefits, promotion or status changes, greater employment security, and a sense of achievement from better performance. Managers are in the best place in the organisation to make this happen. They can also ensure that employees understand the objectives before any training commences and the criteria that will be used to measure success.

People learn at different rates

We each have a different pace to our learning and we learn different things at different rates.

Off-the-job training usually has to be conducted at a single speed to ensure that the program is completed within the allotted time. Training on the job, on the other hand, can proceed at the pace of the learning itself. In a group training situation, trainees can become either complacent or discouraged if their learning speeds ahead or falls behind that of others. When carefully guided and encouraged by the manager, individual on-the-job learning should proceed at a pace that ensures effective learning while, at the same time, the employee maintains enthusiasm through a continuing sense of personal achievement.

People learn by doing

People can learn by watching others demonstrate, or by listening to instructors, but they learn more effectively by doing things and practising the desired behaviours. The more active learners become, the more they learn. There's a saying—*I hear and forget, I see and remember, I do and I understand*—which neatly underlines the need for trainees to have opportunities and encouragement to practise their new skills or abilities. However, practising newly acquired skills in an off-the-job training situation—using role plays, for example—is less challenging and less effective than practising those same skills on real work. Of course, there are situations where trainees cannot practise their new skills in real situations—flying aircraft is one example—until the organisation is confident of their proficiency. In these cases, the close support or supervision of a manager or peer group superior is frequently the way that proficiency is built up and assessed.

Learning is improved and increased by repetition and there are usually more opportunities for this on the job than in an off-the-job training situation. In addition, some people will need more practice on some tasks than on others, and some will need more practice than others. The manager on the spot is well placed to assess that need. Similarly, periodic learning is more effective than mass learning—we can all suffer from information overload or training indigestion—so on-the-job learning that takes place between periods of actual work will be more productive and give learners better opportunities to use their new skills and behaviours before the next stage of training occurs.

Reinforcement and feedback are critical

The employee's manager is in the best position to provide feedback and reinforcement in the learning process. The use of feedback in the performance discussion is described on pages 130–1: the same approach and techniques can be used on the job, probably with a greater likelihood of success. Feedback is more effective when given close in time to the event or behaviour it concerns. Moreover, feedback on a specific event or behaviour is more useful than generalised feedback and enables the employee to change or adjust the behaviour immediately and try a different approach.

Reinforcement involves the use of rewards and punishments to shape learning or behaviour. Rewards are positive reinforcement and increase the chances that an employee will behave that way in the future. Punishments are negative and weaken the probability of repetition. Most important, however, rewards for desired behaviour reinforce learning to a greater degree than punishment discourages undesirable behaviour.

Rewards can be tangible—in the form of promotion or increased pay, for example—but are usually controlled by the organisation according to predetermined policies and procedures. Intangible rewards—such as genuine and public praise or recognition—can be very powerful and effective as reinforcement, and are almost always immediately available to the manager, require no higher approvals and cost nothing but a little time and effort. A 'Well done' or 'You're making really good progress here' comment from the manager is positive reinforcement for the trainee, and lets everyone in the work group know that good performance will be recognised.

At the same time, managers are usually well positioned on the job to pick up inaccurate activity or incomplete learning when it occurs, and can correct undesirable behaviours before repetition gives them any reinforcement. They can also provide employees with information on their results, which is always useful reinforcement for learning. People who are learning need feedback on their progress and performance; they want to know what is expected of them and how well they are doing. Feedback also affects learners' motivation: those who know they are improving are encouraged to continue, while others can become frustrated, angry or discouraged by a lack of information and comment.

Whole learning is usually preferable to part learning

Learning is faster and more effective if learners can see and understand the whole task or process, rather than face a series of small parts of the subject matter. This can usually be done on the job without much difficulty, and learners can see not only the inputs and outcomes but also the processes that are used and the relationships that exist, and they can talk to the people involved.

Having gained the 'big picture' in this way, learners will understand better how their parts of the operation fit into the whole and will probably be more committed to their particular piece of the action. Of course, the learning itself should occur in separate and manageable steps which can be learned in their proper sequence as the employee gradually becomes acquainted with the whole task and gains the competencies needed to carry it out.

Learning must be applied on the job

It is depressing for trainers when course participants concede they are there mainly because the boss sent them and, no, they haven't discussed with their managers why they need this training. It is equally depressing for participants to return to the workplace after a course and be asked if they enjoyed the holiday, followed by 'Now you can get on with some real work!' Learning on the job avoids these two problems, which occur so often with off-the-job training courses.

Managers should ensure that the training courses and development programs that employees undertake are related to the needs of both the employees and their jobs, and focus on equipping trainees with skills and knowledge that will lead to new or changed behaviours on the job. Managers should also brief staff carefully before they undertake any training, explaining why the training is needed and how the learner is expected to benefit. Afterwards, they should discuss how well the training achieved its objectives and what impact it will have on individuals' job performance, and should follow up frequently in the period after the trainee returns to the workplace.

Adult learning

In addition to the general principles of learning outlined in the previous section, we should review what is known specifically about adult learning.

- Adults look for learning that will help them cope with specific events or transitions—for example, a new job, a promotion, redundancy, retirement.
- Adults look for learning experiences because they have a use for the skills or knowledge they hope to learn. In other words, learning is a means to an end, not an end in itself.
- Adult learners are less interested in broad courses than in single-topic learning which focuses on applying the subject matter to relevant problems. They are more interested in solving problems than acquiring knowledge for its own sake.
- Adults need to be able to integrate their new learning with their existing knowledge. It takes them longer to integrate new learning which conflicts with, or does not relate to, existing knowledge.
- Adults take fewer risks in the learning process. Partly because they take mistakes personally, adults are less likely to experiment than to use tried-and-true solutions.
- Adults prefer self-directed and self-paced learning to group learning led by an expert or professional trainer.
- Books, programmed texts, computer-based training and videos are popular with adults, partly because they are 'non-human', partly because learners can use a variety of media, and partly because they can choose when to start and stop.
- Adults want the learning environment to be physically and psychologically comfortable. They dislike long lectures or lengthy periods of sitting, especially if there are no opportunities to practise what they are learning.
- Adults have acquired knowledge and experience and are, therefore, a rich source of information and advice for other learners.
- Adult learning situations must be controlled so that there is an appropriate balance of new material, integration with existing knowledge and sharing of experiences—within the inevitable time constraints. The 'trainer' must be a facilitator rather than instructor, and recognise that people are learning at different speeds, have different levels of existing knowledge, different levels of interest and a range of opinions and experiences.

THE MANAGER AS COACH

For performance development, continuous learning on the job is more powerful than formal off-the-job training courses. It is the responsibility of managers to ensure that work-based learning occurs, which means they must be able to turn workplace incidents and problems into learning opportunities. At its most straightforward, this means that all managers need coaching skills.

Most of us have some idea of the coaching process from the sporting world, but still find it hard to define the term. Essentially, coaching is a one-to-one process: the coaching may be given to an employee by the manager, a colleague or a specialist. But the communication in coaching is two-way, concerned with discussion, discovery and understanding rather than the simple transfer of information or skills. Also, coaching has a problem-solving focus. As shown in Figure 7.1, it is a process for turning workplace problems into learning opportunities.

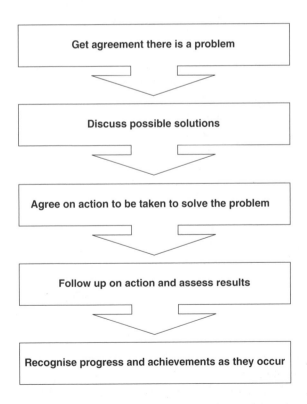

FIGURE 7.1   COACHING FOR CHANGE

Coaching is not a substitute for other forms of training and development. It should be seen as an on-the-job supplement which helps to improve the application of skills and knowledge that employees obtain on or off the job, and which helps them to solve problems so that they can perform better. Because coaching uses everyday incidents as the occasion for learning, the new skill or knowledge can be applied immediately, observed and checked by the manager, and appropriate feedback given.

Alan Mumford (1993) reminds us that responsibility for developing others is not an 'add-on' or 'optional extra' for managers: it is an integral part of the management process. But most managers need to be helped to recognise the learning potential of ordinary situations. He uses this example.

> A customer phones with a quality problem arising from a recent major delivery. 'We want you to send out your production manager and quality manager so that they can see the reality of the problem from the customer's side.' The production manager decides to take a graduate trainee along as well, saying, 'Keep your eyes open, take notes, and we'll talk about it afterwards.'

Mumford says the best way to help managers help others is to get them to think about the experiences from which they have learned. Ask managers to identify their two most helpful learning experiences, and the two least helpful, and to describe what they learnt, and how. Later, they can be asked to think of an experience of being helped by another manager. What was the experience, and what did the other manager do that you found helpful?

Not all managers make good coaches, just as not all managers are good leaders. Edwin Singer (1979) describes the six main characteristics of good coaches.

- They are interested in their people.
- They look for potential.
- They know the interests, desires and capacities of their people.
- Their interests are person-centred rather than work-centred.
- They show confidence in subordinates but expect it to be justified.
- They do not do their subordinates' thinking for them.

Perhaps the major challenge facing the manager who wants to be an effective coach is, once again, the duality of the twin roles of judge and helper. When observing and supervising employees' performance, the manager is in the role of judge. But, as coach or helper, the manager tries to work closely with employees to improve their job performance.

How good a coach are you?

Decide what coaching means to you and how it relates to your work. It may help to think about times when you are helping others with their work problems. For each question, choose the answer that best describes your current style and then check your score.

1. During a typical month, do I spend at least two hours developing each of my staff?
   a. Rarely
   b. Occasionally
   c. Usually
   d. More than two hours

2. Do I:
   a. plan in advance specific coaching assignments or learning opportunities for my staff?
   b. keep an eye open for situations that I can use for coaching purposes?
   c. allow my staff to learn by experience that comes their way in the normal course of business?
   d. deliberately create coaching situations, even at the expense of some immediate operational efficiency?

3. When I am away, who does my work?
   a. Someone does the urgent things—the rest can wait.
   b. My boss.
   c. My staff.
   d. Nobody—only I can do it properly, so it waits until I return.

4. If the performance of a staff member clearly indicates a weakness in an area where I have special expertise, I am likely to:
   a. tell the employee exactly what should have been done and ensure that someone gives close supervision next time
   b. avoid giving the employee that kind of work in future
   c. send the employee on a course
   d. get the employee to do another job of the same kind, ask for regular progress reports, and review and discuss problems as they arise.

5. If a member of my staff comes and asks me what to do about a problem that has come up in a delegated task, do I:
   a. tell the employee to come back in a few days when I have had time to think about it?
   b. say politely that it is the employee's job to find the answers, not mine?
   c. tell the employee what to do?
   d. ask the employee for ideas on what should be done, and how?

Scoring
Use this grid to score your answers and then total your score. If your score is close to the maximum (20), you already have a positive approach to coaching. Those who have lower scores can go back to individual questions to identify areas where their performance might need to improve.

	a	b	c	d
1	1	2	3	4
2	4	2	1	3
3	3	1	4	2
4	3	1	2	4
5	3	2	1	4

Mentoring

As both role and process, mentoring is similar to coaching. It differs in that coaches are usually the employee's direct manager or team leader while mentors come from elsewhere in the organisation or from outside. Kram (1985) describes a mentor as a manager who is experienced, productive and able to relate well to a less experienced employee. The mentoring relationship is intended to be supportive and non-threatening. It is usually informal, although many organisations have formal mentoring programs for their employees, especially those in professional and technical roles or in situations where project-based employment means that few employees get to build strong work-group relationships or one-on-one relationships with managers. According to Carroll et al. (1987), the mentor provides advice related to the protegé's job, career aspirations and development, clarifies misunderstandings and ambiguities the junior person might encounter, builds confidence in the protegé and encourages him or her to take developmental steps that might otherwise not have been risked. The mentor also serves as a sounding board . . . and often acts as the champion of the protegé's career interests among the higher level of incumbents of the organisation.

Feedback and coaching

Many of the communication skills that managers use in the performance review discussion (see Chapter 6) are also needed for effective communication on the job. In particular, feedback and coaching are closely related. Feedback consists of information that describes employees' performance, while coaching is the help they get to improve their performance when the feedback indicates that is what they should do.

The feedback and coaching cycle (see Figure 7.2) begins when performance plans are agreed and continues until the performance review is held. To some extent, both feedback and coaching continue during the

FIGURE 7.2   THE FEEDBACK AND COACHING CYCLE

performance discussion, although their purpose then is less developmental than to summarise what has been happening.

Managers usually find it more difficult to provide effective coaching than effective feedback. For most of us, it seems easier to tell people what is right and wrong than to help them identify what they might do to improve performance or correct a problem. Effective coaches have to be good problem solvers, because coaching is basically problem-solving applied to performance issues.

COACHING FOR PERFORMANCE IMPROVEMENT

From time to time, a manager will decide to provide coaching to solve a particular performance problem. As with a performance discussion, the manager needs to plan the coaching discussion carefully. The manager's plan might follow this pattern.

1. **Set out the purpose of the discussion**
   Be direct and specific. Identify the tasks or behaviours you want to discuss so that there is no confusion about the purpose of the meeting.
   - *I want to talk with you about how you write up your reports on client meetings.*

2. **Describe the performance problem**
   Plan ahead what you want to say. Set it out in observable and measurable terms. Describe what performance you expect or need, what is actually happening, and the effects this is having on the successful completion of the job.
   - *We need to have your reports on the same day or the day after you meet the clients so that the service department or the warehouse or whoever can be told of any problems. At the moment, some of your reports are coming in more than a week after the meeting, and during that time we have clients telephoning to ask when the action you promised will happen.*

3. **Get the employee's reaction**
   Ask for the employee's reaction or comment. Is your description and analysis accurate? If not, how would the employee describe what is happening? Focus the discussion on the tasks or behaviours you have already identified. Ask for the employee's agreement.
   - *How do you feel about this situation?*

- *Do you agree with my assessment?*
- *How do you feel about your performance in this area?*

4. **Analyse the reasons for the unsatisfactory performance**
Discuss the possible causes of the performance problem with the employee. Ask what factors within the employee's control could be contributing to the problem. Try to identify any factors outside the employee's control that might be affecting performance.
- *Why do you think this is happening?*
- *Is it your responsibility?*
- *Who else is involved?*
- *What else is going on that might be affecting the situation?*

5. **Try for a collaborative solution**
Ask the employee for ideas about how to solve the problem. Consider all ideas. Listen. Be patient. If the employee has no useful ideas, have a course of action ready to suggest and ask the employee to respond. But don't lead off with your proposed solution, or impose it. Summarise the actions to be taken, agree who is to take them, and by what date or time.
- *How do you think we might solve this problem?*
- *How would that work?*
- *How would you feel about . . .?*

6. **Assistance and follow-up**
Find out what help the employee will need to implement the agreed actions. Be specific about the assistance you will provide. Identify what each of you will do for follow-up and review.
- *What information or assistance are you going to need to make this work?*
- *Can we agree to meet every two weeks to check progress?*
- *When would you expect to have the problem fixed?*

THE PERFORMANCE DEVELOPMENT DISCUSSION

Why should the discussion of personal and career development be separate from the performance planning and review discussion? Again, the answer lies in the manager's incompatible roles of judge and helper. You might think that more open and collaborative management styles, and the change in the performance discussion's emphasis from appraisal to problem-solving would make the separation unnecessary. And you could argue that performance changes cannot be sensibly planned without discussing the behaviour changes needed to achieve those plans. Whether these concerns are real will depend on the particular objectives and style of your organisation's performance management system.

There are, however, other reasons why discussion of personal or career development should be kept separate from performance planning and review. The first of these relates to time frames. Usually, performance targets are set with relatively short time horizons, seldom more than twelve months. Any essential skills and knowledge training should be planned at the same time and carried out very quickly so that the employee can meet the agreed targets. But discussions of an employee's development paths and options need a broader perspective: they'll go far beyond the skills and knowledge required for particular tasks and won't fit easily within the time frames of performance planning and review.

Second, few managers are equipped to assist employees with longer-term performance development planning. Many of them are not even sure how or where employees might get the training they need for short-term performance improvements. Very few managers have skills in career development and counselling. As a result, performance development discussions are usually restricted to the immediate situation, or the manager's attempts to help employees with their longer-term development are, unintentionally, limiting rather than liberating. Few managers have the skills to help employees assess their strengths and weaknesses and examine their preferences. They lack the information and experience that would enable them to help employees consider a wide range of options and opportunities. Advising a top-performing employee that future career development might lie beyond the present organisation, for example, would be a challenge for most managers.

A third reason for separating performance review and performance development discussions is that their content is different, even if linked (see the example on pages 161–6). The review discussion is concerned with the achievement of job-related plans and targets; the development discussion will examine individual strengths and weaknesses, career aspirations and possibilities, and longer-range personal planning— all aimed at individual development rather than current job performance.

Randell (1989) goes a step further. He describes three different review categories—*reward*, *potential* and *performance*—and argues that there should be separate discussions for each of them. As we see in the next chapter, there's a particularly strong case for keeping remuneration decisions separate from the process of performance planning and review.

In practice, many organisations cover both performance planning and review and performance development in a single discussion. Many of them simply have not thought about the conflict between the manager's roles as judge and helper. Others argue that it is difficult to get managers to carry out one interview, let alone two; in my opinion, they should question whether it's worth those managers doing even one! They argue also that any discussion of future options and development plans needs to be linked to current performance if it is to be realistic for both the organisation and the employee. Some acknowledge the duality of the discussion, and try to overcome it by providing separate forms for performance review and performance development.

Whatever the organisational practicalities, the evidence is clear that performance management systems that try to do too many things end up doing none of them very well. It is clear also that appraisal and development are uncomfortable companions.

Performance development—an example

A finance sector organisation has separate systems for performance planning and review and personal development. But it stresses that the two processes are interrelated:

> The performance review analyses outputs achieved in terms of objectives set at the beginning of the year. The focus of the development review is on individuals, and on developing the knowledge and experience they bring to their roles.

In the personal development review, employees and their managers are expected to formalise a personal development plan. This is described as 'a series of activities which aim to maximise employees' achievements and contribute towards their objectives. The plan may comprise books to read, projects to complete, people to talk to, courses to attend, and so on.

For employees, the development review is an opportunity 'to influence your personal development and take some initiative in this process'. Employees are given a blank personal development review form together with a booklet setting out the key success criteria for their particular job areas. They are asked to prepare for the review by drafting responses to the questions asked in the form. Managers use the same form to prepare for the review. An adapted version of the form is set out over the page.

A Bank Limited
Performance development review

1. List the strengths which you have/the employee has shown in the job over the last year. ....
....
....
....
....

2. Note any areas in which you need/the employee needs to improve job performance. ....
....
....
....
....

3. Consider your/the employee's skills and abilities. Identify any skills or abilities that are not fully used in the present job. ....
....
....
....
....
....

Management abilities and success criteria

Here is a list of the key abilities that lead to success in corporate management positions in a Bank. Detailed definitions are found in the accompanying booklet. Start by thinking about each of the definitions, specifically in relation to your job/the employee's job. Next, describe briefly how well each ability is being demonstrated and rate it using this scale.

5 = Excellent
4 = Commendable
3 = Fully satisfactory
2 = Marginal
1 = Unsatisfactory

Finally, decide whether each of these abilities has high, medium or low priority for success in this position.

Key management abilities	Rating	Priority
1. Basic knowledge of the job *(as an example, the definition is set out on page 165)*		
2. Knowledge of the organisation and its business		
3. Proficiency with the organisation's technology and systems		
4. Thinking, reasoning and information-processing abilities		
5. Seeing the big picture		
6. Clarity of purpose and strategy		
7. Creativity and initiative		
8. Delivering what is expected		
9. Integrity and credibility		
10. People management		
11. Communication		
12. Self-confidence		
13. Client orientation		
If you wish to suggest other criteria which are important for this job, please do so		
14.		
15.		

Development plan

1. Write down the two or three areas of ability which have the highest priority for your/your employee's development.

....

....

....

....

....

....

2. Note specific activities that could help to develop those areas of ability. Consider:
   - projects to be worked on
   - people to talk with
   - books to read
   - videos to view
   - workshops, seminars, courses to attend
   - on-the-job coaching
   - points to remember

Ability area ....

Action(s) to take   *Target date/Time frame*

....
....
....

Ability area ....

Action(s) to take   *Target date/Time frame*

....
....
....

Ability area ....

Action(s) to take   *Target date/Time frame*

....
....
....

Ability area ....

Action(s) to take   *Target date/Time frame*

....
....
....

Ability area ....

Action(s) to take   *Target date/Time frame*

....
....
....

The performance development review is scheduled to take place midway between the employee's performance planning and performance review discussions. This separates the performance and development discussions in time, and also ensures that there are regular, reasonably formal review meetings between managers and employees to supplement, not supplant, their day-by-day interactions on the job.

Each of the eleven areas of management abilities is given a detailed definition in the booklet that employees receive with the form. As an example, this is the definition for *Basic knowledge of the job*.

- Knows and understands basic concepts necessary to carry out the job and has the technical skills to perform competently, e.g. banking, legal and technological skills. Knows appropriate procedures and practices, and is aware of and up to date with industry and market trends in area of expertise.
- A rating of *Excellent* is appropriate when the employee's skills and knowledge are used to deal successfully with all the issues that arise; when situations where practices and procedures should not be followed are identified; and when others are coached to ensure that they understand concepts and practices.
- A rating of *Unsatisfactory* is appropriate when job-related activities are dealt with in such a way that they conflict with the job function and do not support it; where practices and procedures are followed for their own sake rather than to contribute to the job function.

Using these descriptions of job-related and performance-based behaviours links the development review process to the system of performance planning and review. However, the focus of the development discussion is on the employee's abilities and not on the achievement of specific targets.

Note that employees are not asked to speculate about their long-term ambitions: 'What job would you like to be doing in five years?' or to contemplate changes in occupational direction: 'How would you feel about a move into marketing?' This recognises that most employees and their managers have insufficient knowledge about the organisation to discuss longer-term possibilities sensibly. Employees will wonder how wise it would be to express their interest in having the boss's job in five years' time. Or they are allowed to build false expectations by showing interest in an unlikely career move and the manager hasn't the knowledge, or the heart, to counsel them to be more realistic. Career development is discussed in more detail on pages 169–72.

Clearly, the purpose of this review is to encourage employees to think systematically about their development needs in a performance-related context. At the same time, it places an onus firmly on managers to accept and play their role as performance developers. An important aspect of the manager's role as developer is the need to keep reminding employees that their work experiences are learning experiences as well. At the same time, managers themselves have to remember that work problems can be turned into learning opportunities.

HANDLING PERFORMANCE PROBLEMS

When employees perform up to standard and meet expectations, managers have few problems—except, perhaps, in deciding how to reward this performance and encourage it to continue. Similarly, managers have little difficulty handling situations where sub-standard performance results from machinery breakdowns, late deliveries of raw materials or other technical hitches. But when an employee's performance falls below the required level or standard, or the employee fails to achieve agreed performance targets, many managers cope badly—or not at all.

Many do nothing: they ignore the problem in the hope that it will go away. Others react too strongly: they focus on finding fault and blame and criticise the employee concerned, thus damaging the personal relationship they will need to use to fix the problem. Others label the employee as the cause of the problem—'Everyone knows he's lazy' or 'She's hopeless with numbers'—and thus decide that nothing can be done. In fact, there shouldn't be any *problem people* in an organisation—but there will almost certainly be *people with performance problems.*

Performance problems must be dealt with, and dealt with quickly and appropriately. It might not be pleasant or easy to confront poor performers with their problems. We often avoid doing it by understating the seriousness of the problem: 'Nobody will notice a couple of small typing errors' we tell ourselves. But that doesn't solve the problem. Worse, it can give employees the impression that standards don't have to be met—that the organisation talks about performance targets and standards but doesn't really take them seriously.

It means also that managers miss their opportunity to discover whether the employee has a *performance problem* or a *personal problem*. Both need to be dealt with, by focusing on specific instances of underperformance or unacceptable performance. It can be tempting to make excuses for the performance shortcomings of employees who have personal problems. But the failure to deal with the performance problems that result from employees' personal problems gives them no help or incentive to deal with their personal problems—and the performance problems remain.

However, managers should take care not to act simply because people perform differently from others. If their performance is up to standard, targets are achieved, quality requirements met, there is no abnormal call on resources and the work group is not adversely affected, managers should just accept the differences. The first law of delegation is that other people will often do things differently from the way you would. But does it matter? Managers should take action only if it does matter.

What we must do is distinguish between people who are *unwilling* to perform as required and those who are *unable*. Managers need to handle the unwilling and the unable in different ways. In both cases, however, the path to performance improvement starts with the gathering of information.

Performance review discussions can tell us who is performing below the expected level and by how much, but may not disclose why. Unless they have the proper skills for handling performance difficulties, managers may try to guess why there is a problem, and will often be wrong. The problem might be lack of skill rather than lack of effort; or the employee might be unclear on the direction to be taken but not short on motivation; or circumstances unrelated to the employee might have hindered performance. In other words, incorrect assumptions about the 'why' of employee behaviour can lead managers into inappropriate action.

A fear of making the employee upset or angry is perhaps the most common reason why managers avoid dealing with performance problems. Nevertheless, managers have to ignore any personal feelings about the employee concerned, deal with the situation fairly, encourage the employee to accept both the nature and the impact of the problem performance, and try to get the employee to take responsibility for solving the problem. Describing the unsatisfactory behaviour and its effects in a factual and non-judgmental way, supported by a range of examples, will help to keep the focus off the person and on the problem.

An approach to handling performance problems is outlined on the next two pages.

Guidelines for handling performance problems

Is there a problem?
- What are the indications that there is a problem?
- How long has it been a problem?
- How general is the problem?
- How will you know when the problem is solved?

What is the problem?
- Who is the employee with the problem?
- What is the desired action?
- What specifically is being done incorrectly?

Is it an important problem?
What impact does the incorrect performance have on:
- the product or service? . . . quality? . . . cost? . . . quantity?
- the organisation? . . . procedures? . . . image?
- the performer or the performer's department? . . . safety? . . . ease of work?
- other workers or departments? . . . safety? . . . ease of work?

Where has the performance system broken down?
Does the employee
- know that he or she is supposed to take the desired action?
- know what the desired action is?
- know when to take the desired action?
- know how to take the desired action?
  — *If not, provide instruction.*
- know what the desired standard or level of performance is?
  — *If there are no standards, set them.*
  — *If there are standards, make sure that employees know what they are.*
- know whether or not she or he is taking the desired action?
  — *If no, redesign job, provide employee with information and training, observe work performance, give feedback.*
- have adequate resources (e.g. time, equipment) to take the desired action?
  — *If no, provide resources.*
- face any negative consequences for taking the desired action?
  — *If yes, identify and remove negative consequences.*

- face no consequences at all for taking the desired action?
  — *If yes, provide positive consequences.*
- receive immediate, positive consequences for doing something other than the desired action?
  — *If yes, remove positive consequences.*
- receive no information on the consequences of taking the desired action?
  — *If no, provide feedback.*
- receive wrong information on the consequences of his or her actions?
  — *If yes, correct the feedback.*
- receive information on consequences that is insufficient to enable her or him to correct the performance (i.e. not clear, not specific, too late, too infrequent)?
  — *If yes, provide better feedback.*
- know how to interpret information so as to improve or correct the performance?
  — *If no, instruct on how to interpret data.*

Adapted from Rummler (1972)

CAREER DEVELOPMENT

The careers of many people just seem to happen. We move, or get moved, between jobs and occupations and organisations as vacancies occur and opportunities arise, with relatively little thought or planning. It is clear, however, that a close matching of jobs to people leads to satisfied and productive employees. As a result, many organisations see how important it is to provide their key staff, or those who have development potential, with career planning counselling and assistance.

Career planning is a process by which an organisation and its employees identify a sequence of jobs—together with possible learning experiences and necessary training—through which those individuals might progress to fulfil their potential and gain job satisfaction. Career planning should not be confused with *succession planning*, which is the process by which the organisation matches its present staff to its present and future job needs. *Career counselling* or *career advice* involves providing employees with information and assistance so that they can better plan their progress to other positions or roles within the organisation, or to other organisations if the present employer is unable to offer sufficient opportunities in the longer term.

Career development programs offer benefits for both the organisation and its employees. For the organisation, having competent and experienced people contributes to its viability and effectiveness and to the achievement of its business objectives. Planning future appointments and career moves is also essential because of the long lead times needed to train and develop people for new roles and responsibilities. In the short term, career planning and counselling should aim to provide employees with as much information as possible about future career possibilities within the organisation. It should also help employees to understand their strengths and weaknesses and personal aims and aspirations so that they can make better-informed choices when the time comes.

For employees, career planning and counselling give opportunities to gain some influence and control over their future. Rising educational levels and more affluent lifestyles, together with changes in work and life aspirations, make it increasingly difficult for people to be satisfied in their jobs and organisations. For many people, work is no longer the central life focus, but is seen more and more as a means of providing resources or opportunities for other activities. Others are finding it is both possible and acceptable to make significant mid-career changes of job or occupation, sometimes more than once.

While the ultimate responsibility for career decisions rests with the individuals concerned, most need advice and information to ensure that the basis for a decision—especially one involving sudden or dramatic change—is sound. In addition, individuals may not be aware of opportunities to pursue a new career choice or direction with their present employer: sharing that information could avoid the disruption of terminating employment for both employee and employer.

In the short term, career counselling helps employees to develop a greater awareness of themselves and their working environment. It should also help to clarify their job and career preferences. In the longer term, the aim is to assist people to develop their potential and achieve career satisfaction in line with their abilities, interests and aspirations. Employees who take part in these programs need to be willing to confront realities—some of which will emerge during the planning and counselling process—to make plans that are realistic, and to accept that the future success of their careers will be influenced mainly by their own efforts and actions.

At the same time, the organisation must not make promises about future career opportunities if there is any doubt that these will actually occur, or create unrealistic expectations in terms of an individual's abilities and potential, or create demands for training and development that the organisation is unable or unwilling to meet.

Of course, there is a risk that career planning and counselling will help employees to identify any mismatch between their aspirations and the opportunities the organisation can offer, and lead them to seek further career development elsewhere. Yet losing talent that the organisation cannot use properly might not be a real loss, because there is in any case the risk that the employee will become dissatisfied and less productive. Realistically, organisations will always lose some of their better performers. But surely it is better for an organisation to train and develop some who leave than to have no one of real quality coming through? This is not an excuse for losing its talent, and every organisation needs a strategy for retaining its key performers.

Career planning discussions can help staff to be realistic in their ambitions and expectations. It is not unusual for people to expect to reach positions beyond the level that their abilities—or the organisation's circumstances—are likely to take them. It is important for both the organisation and the individual that people have accurate feedback on their performance and potential, so an effective process of performance planning and review is an essential forerunner to career planning and counselling.

Career planning: Do I know what I want?

Think about these questions and then discuss your responses with your family, a friend, a colleague or your manager.

1. Do I know what I do best? What is it? Why?
2. Are there some things that I like to do very much? What are they? Why?
3. Do I work better by myself or with others? What kind of people can I work with? Why?
4. Do I know what talents I don't have? What are they?
5. Do I know the things I dislike doing? What are they? Why?
6. Have I asked for and received advice about what sorts of work I should consider? If yes, what was the advice?
7. Has my education prepared me for these fields? Or do I need further education and training? What do I need?
8. How hard can I work? Physically? Mentally? Can I work long hours?

9. What are my work habits? Do I work intensively in short bursts? Or do I work at a steady pace? Do I know why? What do I prefer?

10. Have I talked with people who do the kinds of jobs I think might interest me? Do I have first-hand information about their work? What is a typical day like for them? What do they tell me?

CHAPTER 8

REWARDING PERFORMANCE

Paying for performance is a big issue in contemporary human resources management. Organisations have long believed that production and productivity improve when pay is linked to performance, and have developed *payment-by-results* (PBR) systems and incentive schemes to support this belief. Expectancy theory tells us that, if people want more pay and believe that working harder will get it for them, they will work harder and perform better. But how to make the theory work in practice has seldom caught people's attention as it does today.

In 1951 the International Labour Office (ILO) defined PBR as wage systems that relate a worker's earnings directly to some measurement of the work of the individual, the group or the work unit. Among benefits the ILO claimed for PBR—which at that time relied heavily on quantitative techniques like work study and industrial engineering—were increased output from improved efficiency, lower production costs, better control of labour costs, less need for direct supervision and more even production flows.

Half a century later, *performance pay* is seen in less mechanistic terms and may be defined more simply as the explicit link of financial rewards to individual, group or organisational performance. According to Brading and Wright (1990) the single most important objective of performance pay is 'to improve performance by converting the pay bill from an indiscriminate machine to a more finely tuned mechanism, sensitive and responsive to the needs of a company and its employees'. It does this by:

- *focusing employees' contributions* where they are of most value, as set out in organisational, business unit and individual performance plans and targets
- *supporting the development of a performance-oriented culture* in which people are paid for results rather than for the time or effort they put in
- *emphasising individual performance or team work as appropriate*: group-based performance pay schemes are used to foster cooperation within the group while personal schemes focus on the contributions made by individuals

- *strengthening the performance planning process*: performance targets and standards carry more significance if performance accomplishments have an influence on remuneration decisions
- *rewarding the right people*: high rewards go to high performers rather than paying everyone around the average
- *motivating all employees*: even those who do not benefit directly see that high performance is appropriately rewarded.

Critics, on the other hand, charge that the use of performance pay to change the behaviour of individual employees, and the organisation as a whole, undermines other human resources programs and their contributions. In particular, say the critics, an emphasis on performance pay can encourage people to focus on short-term results and benefits, to the detriment of the organisation's long-term effectiveness. Instead of rewarding past performance, goes the argument, the organisation should focus on future development, using a range of human resources practices to lead and support the achievement of individual and organisational goals over the long term.

Perhaps most telling, research into individual PBR schemes in the United Kingdom doesn't show that they have any effect on performance. Instead, writes John Purcell (2000), 'the growing conviction is that a pay system can at best have no effect on performance, but, at worst, it will damage competitiveness'. He goes on to say that the idea of linking pay to performance is based on the questionable assumptions that:

- organisations are rational, top-down, decision-making structures
- managers have the foresight to know what is best for the forthcoming year
- people need incentives to get them to behave in a particular way.

Purcell's doubts are not new. There was research evidence more than a decade ago that the introduction of performance pay does not lead to high organisational performance: poor performing companies are just as likely to use performance pay schemes as the most successful (Bevan & Thompson 1991). Nor, according to the Institute of Manpower Studies (Thompson 1992), is there any correlation between performance pay and improved profits: the linkages are more subtle.

The term *performance pay* is usually applied to arrangements where performance and financial rewards are directly linked—such as merit pay, individual incentives and group or organisational bonuses. These techniques are criticised because their focus on financial rewards is said to draw attention away from other forms of organisational rewards, some of which might be more powerful than money itself. This is why some organisations prefer schemes where rewards and individual or team performance are less directly linked—profit-sharing arrangements and employee share purchase plans, for example—but there is no real evidence that they lead employees to take a longer-term view of the organisation's interests.

For the organisation, the system of rewards and remuneration should support the achievement of business and other objectives; for the individual employee, it should satisfy economic needs as well as personal needs for recognition, appreciation, influence and participation, skills development and career progress. And the system has two objectives: to provide *rewards* for past performance and to offer *incentives* for future performance.

Performance in this context includes *behaviour*; it is not limited to *outputs* or *outcomes*. Increasingly, employers are using rewards and remuneration to influence and acknowledge desirable employee behaviours such as innovation and creativity, concern for quality and excellence in customer service. Performance pay can be used to reward these behaviours but will probably be more effective if specific standards and expectations have first been set for these areas.

PERFORMANCE AND REWARDS

The *performance–rewards exchange* is at the heart of the employment relationship. Organisations employ people to perform specified activities to an acceptable level or standard and, in return, employees receive rewards. Those rewards come in two broad categories.

- *Intrinsic rewards* are internal reinforcements (e.g. feelings of accomplishment and self-worth).
- *Extrinsic rewards* are external reinforcements (e.g. pay, other benefits, promotion or recognition).

Extrinsic rewards take two forms: *money* or *non-money* rewards. A well-designed job (see Chapter 2) and a positive organisational culture will provide employees with a range of non-money rewards. Employees can also gain both incentives and rewards—and their opposites—from their personal and working relationships with managers, team leaders and other members of the work group. Beer (1984) tells us that

> intrinsic rewards and extrinsic rewards are both important and not directly substitutable for each other. Employees who are well-paid for repetitious, boring work will be dissatisfied with the lack

of intrinsic rewards; just as employees paid poorly for interesting, challenging work may be dissatisfied with their extrinsic rewards.

Thus, a well-designed, purposeful and challenging job will enable employees to develop their skills and talents, and a working environment that supports individuals and encourages strong interpersonal relationships can build employees' commitment and their contribution to achieving the organisation's goals. However, these factors will not be enough by themselves.

Money rewards—'tangible' rewards might be a better term since many of these rewards do not actually take the form of cash—might be more important in the performance–rewards exchange than non-money rewards. In fact, wages and salaries have traditionally been the major inducement for people to take up work opportunities, whatever theorists say about the role of money in motivation.

But this is a complex and continuing argument. In Abraham Maslow's ascending hierarchy of needs, money is essential for us to satisfy our lower level needs but is only one means of achieving satisfaction at higher levels. For Frederick Herzberg, wages and salaries are a hygiene factor: we may be dissatisfied if we're not happy with our earnings, but don't necessarily feel satisfied with our employment if we feel well paid. And, as long ago as 1922, Elton Mayo showed that letting people schedule their own work would bring dramatic productivity increases where incentive payment schemes had failed.

Managers are often criticised for believing that money is the most important motivator for employees. Yet, for some groups of workers, the managers could be right. In one survey, money was rated as most important by three groups: people under the age of 30, those on low incomes and those at lower organisational levels. Generally, however, employees in the survey rated interesting work, appreciation of their efforts, feeling 'in on things' and job security ahead of good wages (Kovach 1987).

Despite the portrayals of money as only one factor in motivation, it seems to loom very large in the total picture. Why? An obvious answer is that money is important because it is the means we use to meet our various social and economic needs. Second, money is a key part of the basic reciprocal of the employment relationship: workers provide their labour and employers pay a price for it. Moreover, remuneration plays a significant part in our decisions to stay in a job or take a new one.

In the same context, organisations and managers tend to place particular emphasis on the importance of remuneration, partly because it is tangible and partly because it is relatively easy to manage and manipulate. McClelland (1967) suggests that managers think money is a primary and effective motivator because most of them are highly achievement-oriented and attach special significance to money and other tangible rewards. These people are strong believers in steeply increasing financial rewards for greater accomplishment, says McClelland, but are mistaken in believing that money incentives necessarily spur other people. This might also help to explain why, in recent years, many company directors and top executives seem to have become insensitive to the negative impact their remuneration levels and arrangements have on people in the organisation and community generally.

Remuneration can be seen to have an important symbolic role in letting people know how well they are doing and how well they are regarded. But managers find money an easily manipulated item in their relationship with employees, and one that can be handled in a relatively impersonal way. In other words, managers may use money to do the talking in circumstances where it would be more effective and less costly for them to give direct and personal recognition to an individual's contributions and performance.

EQUITY AND EXPECTANCY

Equity theory says people are motivated by a desire for fairness; we want to be treated fairly, so we compare our efforts and rewards with those of other people and use these comparisons to judge whether we are being treated fairly. If we believe our treatment is not fair, we'll take steps to restore our feelings of equity. If we feel unrecognised or under-rewarded and can't do anything about it, we're likely to become dissatisfied, less productive, absent more often and uncooperative in the workplace. On the other hand, if we feel over-rewarded in comparison to others, we're likely to work harder or perform better until the feeling of equity is restored—or we'll rationalise the situation by pretending that we were, in any case, underpaid.

Expectancy theory argues that high motivation and, consequently, high levels of effort will exist when employees see a link between effort, performance and rewards. Other theories of motivation assume that people will behave in ways that enable them to meet their goals and satisfy their needs, but expectancy theory does not accept such a straightforward link between behaviour and goals.

One attraction of expectancy theory is its recognition that different people place different values on different goals. The key point here is that employees must want and value the available rewards; they must believe that those rewards are linked to performance and that their efforts can result in that performance. Guest (1984) says managers can use the features of expectancy theory to provide high motivation for employees.

- Systematically identify the goals and values of the workforce.
- Use that data to design human resources systems that give employees the rewards they want and value, and to show managers how to recognise and reward employees and their performance in the workplace on an ongoing basis.
- Provide rewards on an individual rather than general basis. A general pay rise will have little motivational impact because the relative position of employees remains unchanged. However, selective individual increases linked to performance or contribution or behaviour will provide rewards for some, incentives for others and wake-up calls for those who are not meeting requirements or expectations.
- Make rewards public so that all employees can see a link between good performance and higher rewards. This doesn't mean that salary lists should be pinned up on notice boards, but that significant achievements should be recognised and celebrated throughout the organisation as a way of influencing employee expectations about rewards and incentives.
- Ensure that employees have the knowledge, skills and understanding they need to convert motivation into high performance. There is little point in being willing yet unable; that leads to frustration and lower performance.

LINKING PAY TO PERFORMANCE REVIEW

The emphasis on pay for performance has put more focus on the link between performance reviews and remuneration decisions. Obviously, if the organisation says that pay decisions are based on performance, then the assessment of an employee's performance must be seen to influence that person's remuneration. But there are good reasons to have reservations about such promises.

- Many organisations have performance appraisal systems which managers and employees alike regard as weak and unreliable. If you don't have faith in the appraisal system, why would you have confidence in pay decisions based on those appraisals? If there is to be a direct link between performance reviews and pay, the organisation needs to ensure that its performance planning and review system is designed for this purpose, and that the link is clear and clearly understood.
- However strong the emphasis on performance planning and review,

organisations actually pay people for more than their performance. They reward employees for service and loyalty, for organisation membership and cooperation, and for their skills and knowledge— and each of these is a valid input to remuneration decisions. As we have seen, there are many jobs where the objective is to reach a specified level of performance in a short time and then maintain that performance. A job holder in this position whose performance is fully satisfactory, but whose pay increases depend on perform- ance improvements, would soon be very dissatisfied with the lack of recognition.

- Performance planning and review tends to focus on areas for change or improvement in an individual's performance. In fact, many reviews make no mention of those areas of a job where the employee's performance is quite satisfactory and up to the required standard, and where improvement is not required and could even be undesir- able. In these situations, performance-based pay decisions will take account of the employee's achievements against agreed targets, but will usually give much less attention—and probably insufficient weighting—to those areas of the job where the employee has contin- ued to perform as well as or better than expected.

- Timing can be a problem if there are delays between the perform- ance, the performance review and the pay decision. It's been said that performance appraisal is a talk about last year's performance, held this year, to determine next year's pay. That might have worked when planning and accounting cycles followed a neat and tidy annual cycle, but it hardly suits today's hectic world. All the research tells us that, to be effective, rewards should be given as soon as possible after the performance they relate to. This means that simple and unsophisti- cated systems which allow managers to make awards quickly—a celebration dinner paid for by the company in the week a big sale is made, for example—might have greater reward and incentive effect than a cash payment made some months later after all the profit calculations are finalised.

- Merit pay increases are usually made within budgetary guidelines or constraints. In times of low inflation, especially, this can have the effect of levelling out the dollar amount of any pay increases so that high performers receive little more than those who performed less well. In any case, many organisations and managers are reluctant to give really big increases to their star performers. Remuneration policies commonly provide a 20 per cent differential between 'outstanding' and 'satisfactory' performers, which seems not to offer great rewards for the stars or much incentive to aspirants. All this can lead employees to have doubts about both the performance review and remuneration systems.

- Inadequacies in the design and use of many appraisal systems produce an odd distribution of performance assessments or ratings, often skewed in favour of employees because managers are reluctant to confront issues of poor performance. This has cost implications if organisations base their remuneration decisions on these ratings. It also sends the wrong signals to employees who are being rewarded on the basis of inaccurate assessments.

- In an attempt to deal with the problem of unreliable ratings, some organisations constrain their remuneration increases or practices within a so-called normal curve of distribution. Individual remuneration decisions made in this way can hardly reflect true merit or performance and will probably jeopardise the credibility of the remuneration system overall. In terms of performance and performance pay, there is nothing wrong with an organisation full of stars or tall poppies—so long as they truly warrant those descriptions—although too much excellence might pose other challenges.

Despite these problems, an organisation that aims to pay for performance must seek to relate pay and performance systematically and reliably. Research shows that employees are more satisfied with pay decisions when they are directly linked with decisions about performance and development. The challenge is to make this relationship close, in both time and causation, without employees taking an unrealistic or defensive view of their performance or development needs if they think their remuneration prospects would suffer otherwise. Again, the manager's dual roles of judge and helper add to the difficulty. It means that performance and development issues must be addressed in such a way that employees do not focus on pay—allowing them and their managers to take an overall view of performance. It is an argument for separating pay decisions and development reviews from performance planning and review discussions.

It is possible that employees say they like performance pay because they expect to benefit. But those expectations might be based on misconceptions. For example, Meyer (1980) found that three-quarters of employees in a major organisation thought they were, on average, performing better than the rest of the staff. The proportion who believed this grew at the upper levels of the organisation. Similarly, Wright (1991) describes a finance company where three-quarters of the employees favoured the introduction of performance pay—yet more than 70 per cent of them were already rated as superior performers and were receiving significant bonus payments!

We might also speculate how high-performing employees would react if told there would be no performance-related payments because a bad year meant the organisation could not afford merit rises or bonuses. Individuals see performance pay systems in terms of their own performance and their own remuneration; they are relatively uninterested in the overall state of the organisation, if only because most of them are unable to have any significant impact on its performance.

EFFECTIVE PERFORMANCE PAY SCHEMES

Successful performance pay schemes seem to have these key features.

- The organisation is not seeking an immediate return, but sees performance pay as part of a package of human resources initiatives designed to improve employee motivation and performance in the long term.
- Top managers are committed to involving employees in the development and introduction of effective and valid performance planning and review processes, and to supporting them with well-resourced training programs.
- The pay system is tailormade for the organisation. Its objectives are linked to the organisation's goals and the criteria for individual rewards are clearly related to factors that are critical to the success of the business.

Unfortunately, many performance pay schemes fail these tests. They are seen as a means of managing the pay bill rather than a way to encourage and reward performance. In particular:

- Organisations fail to communicate their performance pay philosophies to employees.
- Performance pay schemes focus on individual performance, even though the organisation is emphasising team work and cooperation.
- There is very little difference between the rewards employees get from a performance pay scheme and what they would have got with, for example, a service-based incremental system.
- There are complaints that people who got the organisation into trouble—and then got it out of that trouble—are more likely to be rewarded than those who never got it into difficulties in the first place!
- Employees' opportunities to improve performance are limited by external constraints.
- Managers and staff resist systematic performance planning and review, which means that pay decisions are made unsystematically and arbitrarily.

The criticisms of performance pay schemes fall into four groups.

- *Performance is very difficult to measure.* How can an individual's performance be assessed with complete accuracy and confidence? How do you calculate each individual's contribution to group or organisational performance?
- By itself, *money may not be a very good motivator.* In the words of Alfie Kohn (1993), financial incentives buy short-term compliance rather than long-term commitment.
- *Performance pay schemes are used as a substitute for good management.* Managers spend time trying to manipulate performance ratings or incentives rather than focusing on how to manage and develop their employees' performance.
- *Performance pay schemes are expensive* to design, implement and maintain. They do not necessarily hold down pay rises, but may involve additional costs to buy out old labour practices and then not deliver on the promises of improved performance and profitability.

An Institute of Manpower Studies survey of employee attitudes found that performance pay does not motivate employees, even high performers, and can actually 'demotivate' them (Thompson 1992). It found little evidence that performance pay helped to retain high performers, and discovered that employees thought its impact on corporate culture was not particularly positive. In addition, employees were not sure whether their performance pay schemes produced fair rewards, although high performers who benefited from the pay system were, predictably, more likely to be positive than low performers.

TYPES OF PERFORMANCE PAY

There are three main types of performance pay schemes—merit pay, individual bonuses and group bonuses—but newer approaches like gainsharing, competency- and skills-based pay and team rewards are attracting increasing interest.

Merit pay

Merit pay is the most widely used form of performance-related pay. It is simply that part of an employee's pay that is determined on the basis of performance. That determination is made, more or less precisely and more or less systematically, according to the philosophies, policies and procedures of the organisation. When low inflation means there is no demand for substantial across-the-board pay increases, organisations look for ways to assess, measure, recognise and reward genuine differences in people's performance and employees look to merit pay increases to maintain and improve their incomes.

Merit pay has been used for so long that many people scarcely think of it as a type of performance pay. As always, the most obvious techniques may also be the most effective. However, there are some difficulties.

- With many schemes, the merit or performance pay component is added to the employee's existing pay level to create a new base rate. This has the effect of merging the performance-related pay element into normal pay, thus diluting the incentive or reward effect of the merit payment. The employer's overall remuneration costs increase, but without a lasting impact on the employee's motivation. Keeping the performance pay element separate from the base rate has two advantages: first, it clearly signals that performance pay is different from base pay; second, it can be increased or decreased whenever warranted by the employee's performance.

- Concerns about cost lead many organisations to establish tight remuneration budgets in which merit pay increases are given particular scrutiny and often restricted to a dollar amount or a percentage of the total budgeted cost. This means that individual performance is not the sole determinant of merit pay, with performance ratings being manipulated so that consequent merit pay decisions fit within budgetary constraints. All of this is known to employees who, predictably, are cynical. The problems that many managers seem to have in discriminating between individuals on performance grounds may also reduce the motivational value of merit pay.

Individual bonuses

Performance or incentive bonuses may be paid to individuals as lump sums and not absorbed into salary or remuneration. Such payments are usually made on the basis of measurable outputs or results—based on sales figures, production volume or profits, for example. Payments can be made at any time or interval and can thus be related closely to the performance or achievement the organisation seeks to recognise.

Bonuses should be large enough for recipients to see them as significant and, therefore, motivating, which has obvious cost implications. At the same time, bonuses can become part of normal income—losing any particular reward or incentive effect—if the amount or timing takes on a regular pattern. Problems can also arise if some employees get bonuses on the basis of highly measurable performance while others, whose job performance is less quantifiable, have their bonuses based on whole-job appraisals.

Group bonuses

Unlike merit pay and individual bonuses, group bonuses are intended to reward the overall performance of a work group, team, unit or department, or the organisation as a whole. Usually, all employees receive the same cash amount or the same proportion of their basic remuneration as the bonus. It is paid separately from other remuneration—for example, when a project is completed, or at a set time such as the announcement of the year's profit or at the end of the year. However, regular bonuses—an annual Christmas bonus of $100 for all employees, for example—become predictable and expected and have little reward or incentive effect. Generally, it can be questioned whether group bonuses have any positive effect on the motivation of employees as individuals, but they are often paid in addition to individual bonuses or merit pay and might contribute to the overall rewards and incentives pattern.

PAYING FOR PERFORMANCE

There are many ways to convert assessments of people or their performance into decisions about remuneration increases. Some approaches are described here.

Fixed percentage increases

The employee's pay is increased by a previously determined and fixed percentage, according to the employee's performance rating. Managers usually receive financial data before making their performance assessments, which gives them some idea of the possible impact of their pay recommendations or decisions. Some schemes use a matrix approach which incorporates non-performance factors such as length of service.

A simple example is set out here, although it is unlikely that many organisations would give even their best performers an 18 per cent salary hike!

Performance rating	Percentage salary increase
Outstanding	18
Excellent	13
Satisfactory	10
Acceptable	5
Unsatisfactory	0

Range of percentage increases

Managers are given discretion within a range to award percentage increases based on the performance ratings of individual employees. This approach offers more flexibility, although managers must be ready to justify why two employees with the same performance rating receive different increases.

Performance rating	Percentage salary increase
Outstanding	16–20
Excellent	11–15
Satisfactory	6–10
Acceptable	1–5
Unsatisfactory	0

Fixed increments

Organisations with pay systems built on fixed monetary figures or scales often relate their performance-related pay to movements or steps on those scales. However, such systems are not very flexible for rewarding performance and can be seen as a means of providing automatic increases.

Performance rating	Percentage salary increase
Outstanding	3 increments or steps on the scale
Excellent	2 increments or steps
Satisfactory	1.5 increments or steps
Acceptable	1 increment or step
Unsatisfactory	No change

Pay ranges

In many pay systems, especially those based on job evaluation and linked to Management by Objectives performance reviews, fixed or incremental pay scales are replaced by a range for each position or group of positions. The ranges are established through job evaluation and a determination of the market rates for similarly sized jobs. The employee's movement within the range for the position is, nominally, based entirely on performance. The range itself is changed to reflect changes in the organisation's financial performance or the cost of living, labour market conditions and other factors that the organisation considers relevant.

Typically, the pay range for a job might extend 20 per cent either side of a midpoint that represents fully satisfactory performance for that job, and is usually seen as the 100 per cent level. Outstanding performers are paid 20 per cent higher than the midpoint—that is, at 120 per cent of the satisfactory performance level—while trainees, new appointees or unsatisfactory performers are paid at the 80 per cent level (see box below).

Performance level description	Percentage of pay range
Initial salary level for trainees and new appointees; salary level for unsatisfactory performers. Regular performance planning and review discussions are scheduled.	80
Experienced employees who are performing satisfactorily in many key areas of the job and making good progress towards fully satisfactory performance.	90
Fully satisfactory performance in all key job areas. These employees are fully effective in their current roles and no improvement is needed to meet performance targets or standards.	100 midpoint
Experienced employees who, in addition to performing completely satisfactorily in all key areas of their jobs, are often performing above the expected standards or targets.	110
Star employees who constantly exceed the expected performance targets or standards, and who frequently display exceptional creativity or take significant initiatives.	120

In practice, few organisations can stick rigidly to these pay levels without encountering recruitment or retention problems. For example, an organisation which has to pay more than the 80 per cent level to recruit an experienced replacement employee might set up relativity problems with its existing experienced staff in the same position. In other situations, managers will give generous performance ratings or interpret performance requirements liberally, just to give a pay rise to an employee whose performance does not, strictly, justify such an increase. At a more technical level, the use of job evaluation for determining remuneration relativities is increasingly a subject for debate.

Some organisations have problems holding to the 'midpoint' of the salary range as the appropriate pay level for fully competent and fully satisfactory performers. Placing employees in the middle of the range just doesn't seem to be the 'right' position for 'fully competent' or 'fully satisfactory' performance—and assessments or ratings get manipulated to move the salaries for these people into the top half of the range. That problem can be overcome by distinguishing between employees who meet the standards or achieve their targets and those who don't. The box below shows a salary range based on the ratings used for the model performance planning and review format at the end of Chapter 6.

Performance level description	Percentage of pay range
Did not meet job requirements	80–99
Consistently met job requirements and standards	100
Exceeded job requirements and standards at times	101–107
Consistently exceeded job requirements and standards	108–115
Far exceeded job requirements and standards	116–20

There's another point to be made here. In some situations, a change in an employee's job classification, involving a change in the pay range, might be a better move than a performance-related pay increase or bonus. Many outstanding performers are actually undertaking bigger and more important or more responsible roles than their current job descriptions provide. In other words, an outstanding performer might not, in fact, have the same job as other employees, despite job titles and other appearances. Reclassifying that employee into a job with a higher pay range offers increased financial rewards and also provides the employee with recognition, growth and opportunities for even higher remuneration.

Merit and bonus payments

Some organisations have fixed pay scales or ranges for each position and use lump sum bonus or merit payments to recognise performance. The amount of those payments is decided with widely differing precision and methodology.

Because performance-related bonuses or payments do not affect the employee's basic pay level, this approach is particularly useful where individual performance can fluctuate, either up or down. This overcomes the problem that can arise when performance payments are built into a person's pay: they become part of the basic pay level and thus lose any particular reward or incentive effect. In addition, because they are absorbed into the base pay rate, it is difficult to withdraw performance-related payments if performance falls away. Separate performance payments solve that problem, at least in part, because no payment need be made when performance is poor.

Gainsharing

Productivity gainsharing is well suited to environments where team work rather than individual contribution is encouraged. Gainsharing is defined as a managerial strategy for promoting productivity through incentives: employees share in cash bonuses based on the contributions they make towards cost savings and improved performance. Because individual employees feel able to get involved in contributing directly to these improvements, gainsharing or 'added value' plans have an advantage over profit-sharing and employee-share schemes, which are seen as too remote by most workers. It they are to be successful, gainsharing plans must involve employees in target-setting and decision-making, as well as the financial rewards, and so these schemes require a high level of participation, consultation, shared information and joint decision-making. Gainsharing may be seen less as performance pay than as a way to organise and manage people.

Profit-sharing and employee-shareholding plans

Profit-sharing and employee-shareholding are not strictly forms of performance pay, even though they might be part of an organisation's remuneration system. In earlier years, Kanter (1987) and others suggested that profit-sharing plans were part of a trend away from status-based pay towards performance-related pay. That trend may have slowed more recently with adverse publicity for share-option plans for top executives and the uncertainties of the world's share markets. On the whole, financial participation schemes like profit-sharing and employee-shareholding are so remote from individual performance that it is better to see them as additional benefits and an opportunity for employees to share in the organisation's success. Generally, top managers are more interested in equity participation schemes—that is, schemes that confer some degree of ownership, however small. Employees generally, it seems, do not regard the financial rewards of share schemes to be large enough or quick enough, and are not seduced by suggestions that ownership of shares is a form of employee empowerment.

Paying for skills and knowledge

There is nothing new about paying people according to their skills and knowledge. But the concept has attracted renewed interest in recent years—partly because of the difficulties that organisations experience with performance pay, and partly because the focus of human resources programs in many organisations has been shifting from actual performance to potential performance.

In some cases, the change to pay based on skills and knowledge has accompanied a shift towards competency-based approaches to recruitment, selection, training and performance management. In other cases, skills-based pay systems have been developed to help organisations extract themselves from rigid structures of job classifications and wage relativities. And the so-called 'knowledge organisations' argue that their 'knowledge workers' must be paid for what they know, not just what they do.

Skills-based pay schemes are intended to encourage employees to increase their range of job skills and thus become more flexible in the workplace. They reward employees for the number, types and depth of skills they develop, and award pay on the basis of the jobs they are capable of performing rather than on the jobs they are currently allocated. Additional remuneration is gained as employees acquire new skills of use in their employment. But this raises the question of what skills or knowledge will be rewarded: does the organisation pay for all the skills and knowledge the employee might have, or just for those the employee is using at the present time?

Skills-based pay schemes are usually linked to progress from an entry-level or trainee position through to full and effective contribution to the work of the group. Both performance and ability are considered in the assessment of the employee's progress. However, once the employee has acquired the various elements of skill or knowledge and, therefore, reached the highest available earnings level, the question 'What next?' must arise.

The trend towards skills-based pay makes significant additional demands on the organisation. First, it needs to provide continuing access to training programs so that employees are persuaded that the organisation is sincere about skills development and skills-based pay. Second, different methodologies are needed to define jobs and job structures that match the new grading and pay systems. In addition, management needs to be more open and participative in its style, and might need to move in that direction before introducing skills-based pay.

Cross (1992) argues that skills-based pay should not be used when the work environment is unstable and skill requirements can rapidly become redundant, or as a device for increasing pay levels to buy out overtime, or when change is required so quickly that there is insufficient time to introduce training programs and develop understanding and acceptance of the new approach.

Competencies-based pay

Competencies-based pay is a form of skills-based pay. An employee's basic pay and subsequent progression through pay scales is set according to the employee's number and level of competencies. As with skills-based pay, the assumption is that an employee with more and better competencies will make a bigger and better contribution to the organisation. Unfortunately, this assumption is only relevant where the competencies are genuinely needed for the employee's work.

There are five major steps in the development of competencies-based pay schemes; these steps can also be used in developing skills-based pay plans.

1. *Define the competencies* that employees must demonstrate they have mastered in order to qualify for the assigned pay level or range.
2. *Arrange the competencies* in a hierarchy or sequence that clearly shows the differences between groups of competencies and how employees can move from one group to another.
3. *Set the pay level* that employees will be entitled to receive once they have demonstrated their mastery of each group of competencies.
4. *Decide how to assess* employees' competencies.
5. *Provide training* and other programs so that employees can develop their competencies.

Career-based pay

Career development or *career advancement* pay is a variation on skills-based and competencies-based pay. Progression through pay scales is determined by the employee's 'accomplishments' and not by length of service. For example, to move from Grade 2 to Grade 3 an employee might need to demonstrate understanding and skills in certain defined areas, to have been involved in certain kinds of projects or to have undertaken certain types of activities (e.g. team-leading). For this approach to be successful, there must be specific criteria for each step or grade and an individual's advancement must be considered and agreed by a panel, not just one manager.

Paying for team performance

As organisations have turned to teamwork as a way to achieve higher performance, there has been a trend towards performance pay for groups rather than individuals. We have already seen that rewards and remuneration can be used to influence and recognise patterns of working and behaviour; this can happen on a group basis as well as for individuals. However, the problems that bedevil performance pay generally are greatly increased when it comes to designing and implementing performance pay schemes for work teams.

Team rewards

Team-based rewards are payments to members of a formally established team or other forms of non-financial reward which are linked with the performance of that team. The rewards are shared among the members of teams in accordance with a published formula or on an ad hoc basis in the case of exceptional achievements. Rewards for individuals may also be influenced by assessments of their contributions to team results.

Michael Armstrong (1996)

Michael Armstrong (1996) says the purpose of team rewards is to reinforce the kinds of behaviour that lead to and sustain effective team performance by:

- providing incentives and other means of recognising team achievements
- clarifying what teams are expected to achieve by relating rewards to the attainment of predetermined and agreed targets and standards of performance or to the satisfactory completion of a project or a stage of a project
- conveying the message that one of the organisation's core values is effective teamwork.

Organisations told researchers for the UK Institute of Personnel and Development (IPD 1996) that they were developing team-reward processes to encourage group endeavour and cooperation. They thought individual variable pay schemes could prejudice team performance by:

- encouraging individuals to focus on their own interests rather than those of the team
- encouraging managers and team leaders to treat team members only as individuals, rather than relating to them in terms of the team's role and objectives and what they as individuals could do for the team.

Rewards for team performance are discussed in detail in Chapter 9.

PERFORMANCE PLANNING AND REVIEW FOR TEAMS

Teams and teamwork have become popular tools of organisation and management in recent years, raising new issues and challenges for performance planning and review. Inevitably, some people claim that the trend towards team-based working sounds the death knell for performance planning and review. That would possibly be true if performance planning and review techniques could not be adapted to new ways of working. But they can be adapted and many organisations have successfully done so.

Most of us have some concept of teamwork. For many, it's an idea that has grown up over years of experience as players or spectators in the sports arena—a picture of a group of individuals who join together in combined effort for a common purpose. Generally, we don't need to think more deeply than that. In the workplace, however, things are different. This is not the place for a broad discussion of teams and teamwork, but we highlight some particular issues of significance to performance management in a team-based work environment.

Teamwork is not a new phenomenon in organisations and workplaces. In the 1960s and 1970s, for example, the Swedes sparked off worldwide interest with the use of autonomous and semi-autonomous work groups in manufacturing companies, and the Americans attracted similar attention with the emergence of the Quality of Working Life movement. More recently, amid the pressures of changing economies and increasing global competition, teams and teamwork have been embraced enthusiastically by managers seeking solutions to complex dilemmas. As with the wide range of management fads that preceded teamwork, some of the promise of teamwork might have been exaggerated. Kinnie and Purcell (1998) observe:

> Teamworking, it is claimed, can transform organisational performance and attitudes by creating a virtuous circle in which increased employee involvement leads to improved motivation and productivity.

And, according to Slater and West (1995):

> Teamwork enables people to accomplish more together than they would working alone and so, if successful, can be a source of satisfaction at work. In addition, team members can be supported by and learn from others, thus promoting personal and career development.

Performance planning and review, surely, has an important role in helping organisations deliver on the promises of teamwork. However, when it comes to performance planning and review for teams, there are some special challenges. They are the subject of this chapter. But we must start with this caution.

The term 'team' tends to get overworked in organisations. In reality, relatively few workplace tasks or activities are genuinely designed for, or undertaken by, teams. Rather, tasks and activities are carried out by individuals who work together cooperatively, so that the sum of their efforts becomes the achievement of the team's aims and their common purpose. In this sense, 'team' is just the label used to describe a small unit of organisation that needs to have its performance planned and reviewed just like any other part of the enterprise. The modern telephone call centre is an example of a situation where a number of similarly qualified and experienced individuals are employed to do the same job in a group environment. The call waiting at the head of the queue is answered by the next

The case for team performance planning and review

The United States Office of Personnel Management (1998) says managers and team leaders, and team members, can use performance planning and review to

- plan team and individual performance
- set team and individual goals that are aligned with organisational goals
- establish performance expectations
- measure actual team and individual performance against desired performance
- determine developmental and training needs
- provide feedback on performance
- provide a basis for recognising team and individual performance.

available employee, and all employees are trained to respond in much the same way, ensuring as much consistency as possible in the service to customers. But the work is still carried out by individuals, not by the team. It takes more than a new label to make a team out of this group of individuals. But team performance planning and review can help.

In some organisations, every group gets called a 'team'. At best, this is exaggeration. A special task force which meets a few times to undertake a specific assignment is not really a team. Nor is the executive committee that comes together once a month to look at routine reports and oversee the organisation's operations truly entitled to be called, in most cases, a management 'team'.

Thus, in the context of performance planning and review, organisations might think carefully about how they use the terms 'team' and 'teamwork'. They might assign employees to work groups which they then call 'teams', but many of those so-called 'team members' go on doing individual jobs. Many of them have quite different roles from other team members and require quite different knowledge and skill sets. Their so-called 'team leaders' will probably have much the same roles and responsibilities for managing people and performance as their predecessors did, but they were called 'managers'! Not all groups of workers are teams.

Similarly, while organisations might want people to work more co-operatively, that alone will not make a work group into a team: what many organisations want is what David Limerick (1993) calls 'collaborative individualism'. In these situations, where the achievement of 'team' targets depends on the participation and contributions of team members, individual workers continue to need quantitative and/or qualitative work standards and performance targets—the usual stuff of performance planning and review. We will return to this point.

Finally, we have to ask how many organisations recognise the full implications of moving to team-based working. How many organisations change the nature of their support systems to reflect the new way of working?

- Does the team get to make its own policies and operating rules?
- Are performance standards and targets set for the team as an organisational unit in line with the overall operating plans and objectives?
- Is the team paid, at least in part, as a team?
- Are members of the team trained so that they can do the jobs of other members?
- Are team members given the responsibility for hiring, firing, discipline and development decisions?
- Do team members assess the contributions and performance of other team members?

But perhaps more than any of these operational questions, do organisations recognise that the change to team-based working really requires them to adopt new value systems—about where power lies, about how and where decisions are made and about how work and people are allocated and managed? That's a long way from 'collaborative individualism'.

DIFFERENT KINDS OF TEAMS

One team can differ from another team in several ways. We've already noted that lazy use of the term can identify teams that are, in reality, just groups of workers. Teams will also differ in terms of their membership make-up, the nature and complexity of the tasks they undertake, and their interdependence with other groups and units inside and outside the organisation. In a sense, no two teams are alike—which means that, as with individuals, no one system of performance planning and review is likely to fit all teams.

For our purposes, it is sufficient to distinguish two main types of teams.

- **Process teams.** This term can be used to describe intact groups that are engaged in continuous process or repetitive cycle work or services, and are usually close to management and the organisation's support mechanisms. Typically, they undertake the organisation's core work. The production teams in manufacturing assembly plants are a good example of process teams. Its members are full-time and permanent, and have every reason to expect that the team will be permanent as well. The team is a well-developed social system whose members know each other well. They all have similar skills and are trained for most of the activities undertaken by the team. The work itself is routine and standardised, and cycle times are short and repeated many times during the performance planning and review period.
- **Project teams.** These are groups formed for special non-routine purposes or assignments, with members drawn from a range of specialisations to meet the needs of the task. The team members are expected to cooperate and collaborate, because achievement of the team goal requires them to integrate their different expertise and experience, but otherwise they have very little interdependence. Typically, the work has defined start and end points and very clear objectives. Both the work and the team given responsibility for it are usually temporary—for example, the cast and production crew of a movie, the architects, engineers and builders who design and

erect a building, the specialists from different parts of the organisation who develop the manufacturing and marketing plan for a new product. The members might be separated geographically and meet only occasionally or, in the case of 'virtual' teams, perhaps not meet at all. Often, the members of a project team continue with their 'normal' work and devote only part of their time to the team's project.

Inevitably, these groupings are not absolute. Take, for example, the crew of an airliner en route from Singapore to London. It is both a *process team*—in the sense that the members are permanent employees of the airline and this flight is part of a repetitive cycle—and a *project team*—because the flight deck and cabin crew who make up the team for this flight might be working together for the first time and might never again be rostered to work together. Each organisation should look carefully at the true nature of each of its teams. Why? Because different kinds of teams need different kinds of performance plans and measures.

WHOSE PERFORMANCE?

Once the decision is made to use teams as organisational units, they have to be brought into the performance management system somehow. The staunchest advocates of the virtues of teams and teamwork would want you to abandon individual performance planning and review at this point and use only the team for performance management purposes.

Most organisations don't go with that advice. They recognise the importance of individual contributions to team performance. Put another way, they understand that individual performance planning and review for many workers can no longer be focused solely on the formal performance requirements of the individual's job: it must be expanded to include that person's role as an 'organisational citizen' and as a 'team member'. In this way, performance planning and review is concerned as much with inputs and behaviours as with outcomes and results.

There's a further reason for continuing with individual performance planning and review, even when a system of team performance management is put in place. When the skills and effort that individuals contribute to the workings of the team are not assessed and recognised, the likely result is *social loafing*.

This is a 'conscious or unconscious tendency to shirk responsibilities by withholding effort towards group goals while sharing in rewards' (Scott & Einstein 2001). People show fewer signs of social loafing in small teams than in large groups (presumably because it is more evident in the smaller group), but they are more likely to loaf when rewards and recognition are tied to team effort rather than individual effort (Kidwell & Bennett 1993). Subsequently, other team members reduce their level of effort and commitment when the team is forced to carry a social loafer or freeloader.

We can look at this from another viewpoint. In blunt terms, individuals who are not performing well should not be able to 'hitch a ride' on the overall results of a well-performing group. But, if team results are all we review, the freeloader is potentially safe from counselling, discipline or other action—except for any informal retribution that other team members might exact! Encouraging that kind of competitiveness and self-regulation within a team is hardly consistent with the usual reasons we give for introducing team-based working.

Thus, individual performance planning and review can contribute to team effectiveness by providing members with feedback on the appropriateness of their behaviour and on their need to develop the ability to make greater or different contributions to the team. At the same time, team-based performance assessment can help the team to recognise any problems of performance or relationships and to decide how to deal with them.

In fact, there's no question of individual *or* team performance planning and review: you need both. But they might focus on different kinds of performance or contribution.

TEAMS AND INDIVIDUALS

Assessing team performance can be very difficult. It is difficult enough to assess the performance of many employees, especially knowledge workers, on an individual basis. Put several of these specialists together in a project team with a single task or target, and the assessment of performance becomes a huge challenge. As we have seen, it is particularly hard to decide where individual contributions give way to team effort. This continuing ambiguity between team performance and individual behaviour is a reminder that we cannot sensibly plan and review team performance but ignore the contributions of individuals.

There are two dimensions to individual performance in the context of the team.

- **Team membership behaviour.** Individual employees can be assessed for their effectiveness as members of the team. How well does this person work with other team members? How effective is this person's contribution to decision-making and other group processes? How well does the employee share information and insights with other team members? How effective is this person's participation in team meetings? How do the other team members feel about this person? Essentially, the behaviours to be focused on relate to communication and information-sharing and team supportiveness; in the main, they involve interpersonal skills.

Should the 'team membership' aspects of an individual's position be included in a job description? The answer to this question is almost certainly 'yes' for members of process teams (see page 196), but we might be less certain for members of project teams. For them, the answer will depend on how long the employee will be a member of the project team and what proportion of the person's total time and effort will be devoted to the project team's work.

- **Individual contributions and results.** In most cases, it is possible to plan, monitor and review both the quantity and quality of the work that an individual contributes to the overall results of the group. These performance measures and standards will likely be the same as those used for individual performance planning and review—volume and value of sales, proportion of correct and incorrect answers provided, and other indicators of timeliness and accuracy.

Of course, whether it is desirable to plan and review individual contributions to the team in this way is another question. It might be appropriate for the members of project teams—because their contributions to those temporary groupings are part of their overall responsibilities and effort—but entirely inappropriate for the members of process teams, where individual efforts are subordinate to the workings of the team as a unit.

Ideally, when an organisation chooses a team-based approach to work, the focus for performance planning and review is on the performance of the team as well as the contributions of individuals to that performance. If the focus is on individual performance instead of team performance, the available incentives and rewards will work in favour of individual effort and accomplishment, which sets up the risk of individual competitiveness at the expense of team interests.

The links between team-related performance measures and individual performance measures make up the matrix shown on the next page, developed by the United States Office of Personnel Management (1998). It clearly shows how individual team members' inputs have a significant influence on most team outcomes.

Team-related measures matrix

	Behaviours/Process measures	Results measures
Individual level An employee's contribution to the team	Whether or how well the employee: • cooperates with team members • communicates ideas during meetings • participates in the team's decision-making processes	• The quality of the written report • The turnaround time for the individual's product • The accuracy of the advice supplied to the team • The status of the employee's case backlog
Team level The team's performance	Whether or how well the team: • runs effective meetings • communicates well as a group • allows all opinions to be heard • comes to a consensus on decisions	• The customer satisfaction rate with the team's product • The percentage decline of the case backlog • The cycle for the team's entire work process

WHAT PERFORMANCE?

As with individual performance planning and review, we must first decide which aspects of a team's performance are critical to its work and success. There are three possibilities: one concerned with *results and outcomes* or actual performance, one with *behaviours and processes* or how the team performs, and one with *competencies and capabilities* or potential performance. But this discussion should start with a caution.

Organisations introduce team-based working and encourage the development of teams because they see them as tools for improving the effective delivery of products or services. Unfortunately, when it comes to assessing the effectiveness of teams, many organisations select criteria or measures that assess *successful teamwork* rather than *successful work*.

The criteria used for assessing how well teams work—behaviours or attributes like participation, communication and decision-making, for example—can become objectives in themselves, as if the reason for having teams is teamwork, not work. It's not much comfort to a failed organisation to learn that it had achieved a high level of teamwork! So care is needed to ensure that the measures selected for assessing team performance are business-based and truly aligned to the strategies and plans of the organisation.

According to Robert Sahl (1998), team measurements—especially in organisations where variable pay is linked to overall team performance—can and should be a 'unifying force', providing common goals that:

- can and should supersede individual goals
- justify cooperative effort at the expense of purely selfish endeavour
- provide a different paradigm for perceptions of the 'value' of work and workers, for both the organisation and the employees themselves. In other words, team-based organisations are trying to create value systems that are, essentially, opposed to the traditional values of individualism. At the very least, they have to instil the idea that individual interests must be seen as secondary to the interests of the team, because the main role for the individual is to support and improve the performance of the team.

No matter what individual values shape a team member's efforts, sense of achievements and other rewards, says Sahl, there is another level of values that derives from participation in the team. These values are defined by team measurements which, apart from a link to organisational goals, need these distinguishing characteristics.

- **They must be relevant to the team members.** Team standards or targets must relate to aspects of behaviour or performance that team members can themselves control or influence. As with individual performance plans, it is a mistake for teams to have targets remote from their level or reach. Few teams, for example, can directly determine or influence a company's overall financial results; they can, however, have a significant impact on revenues and costs in their own operating areas. This means that the measures of team performance should change as we move down through the levels of the organisation: the top-management 'team' is validly concerned with strategy; teams at the departmental or business unit level can be measured in terms of customer satisfaction, market share, productivity and similar broad criteria; while process teams on the factory floor should be assessed in such terms as cycle time, delivery, quality and waste.

- **They should not be simply an aggregate of individual targets.** Instead, team targets should describe end results that justify having this work done by a team rather than individuals. Thus, 'total sales value' is a meaningless measure if the members of the sales force never talk to each other, but it is a valid measure if the sales team members are constantly swapping market information, sharing sales leads, helping others with demonstrations or paperwork and generally interacting and cooperating.
- **Team targets must be verifiable.** Team targets, like individual targets, should be specific and measurable. But, again like individual targets, this does not mean that team targets must necessarily have numerical or quantitative measures. Descriptive measures may be more appropriate for many team targets—especially those concerned with how the team operates—and are quite valid so long as they clearly set out what evidence is required to determine whether the target has been met.
- **They should, where possible, include points for checking progress.** A team should be able to check from time to time that it is making appropriate progress towards the achievement of a long-term target. We know that individuals can become discouraged if a target appears too remote or unreachable. That hurdle will loom even higher when scaled up for a whole team.
- **Team measures should be clear to all team members, and understood by them.** Communication of team targets and progress towards accomplishment should be a continuing concern for the team itself, and for the team's management support structure. There's no point in having targets if they're not well understood and if people don't know what they have to do to reach them.

Team results or outcomes

A team's performance can be planned and reviewed in terms of results or outcomes; in other words, actual performance outcomes can be compared with the standards or targets set for the team at the beginning of the particular period or project. Typical results-based team measures would include, for example, the proportion of on-time deliveries made by the distribution department, the number or value of sales completed by a marketing team, the achievement of staged deadlines by a product-development task force, and the proportion of incoming calls answered within a specified time limit in a call centre.

The assessment can be done very simply by asking whether the team has met its goals or completed its assigned task. A simple 'yes' or 'no' answer will be adequate for some purposes—for example, deciding whether the team qualifies for a bonus payment or whether a target completion date for a project should be extended—but it's not very informative or helpful.

In many situations, what we need to gather is information about the quantity and quality of the team's outputs—for example, number of completed cases, number of satisfied customers, number of complaints, volume of rejects, total expenditure—so that these results can be assessed in the light of the standards or targets set for the team. The obvious next step is to ask 'why' the team has produced those particular results, especially if the performance has fallen below its set targets or standards. The risk here is that this examination will focus on individual team members and their contributions, rather than on the team as a whole. Of course, that bears out the point that much so-called 'teamwork' is simply a collection of individual jobs.

Results or outcomes are an appropriate measure for performance planning and review for *process teams* (see page 196)—but not for the individuals who make up those teams. Why not? First, if the team is operating as a unit it should be impractical (if not impossible) to identify individual contributions to the overall effort or achievement. Second, even if it were possible to identify individual contributions, it would be unwise—for this would take the focus off the team and put it back on to individuals, thus weakening the proposition that teamwork is something more than the sum of its parts.

Despite the focus on task and task accomplishment, outcome-based performance planning and review is not very useful for *project teams*, if only because they usually cease to exist once the task is completed. What these teams need to plan is a series of regular task-related milestones or checkpoints, so that they can review and assess progress and make any changes that will enhance the team's operations or achievement potential. And, because their nature means that project teams often lack effective leadership, these progress reviews can become an important source of direction, encouragement and (sometimes) discipline for team members.

Team behaviours and processes

Defining the behaviours a team should use to achieve its targets or complete its assignments, and assessing its internal processes and workings offer good scope for team performance planning and review. How well does the team work? How well are its meetings and other group activities planned and coordinated? How well does it operate as a problem-solving unit? Is the team aware of itself as a unit?

In addition, agreed statements or standards of desirable team behaviour establish a framework for assessing the behaviour and contributions of individual team members, especially in terms of cooperative relationships, collaborative communications and other teamwork behaviours. In turn, this allows individual performance plans and review to be related closely to team effectiveness.

Team competencies or capabilities

Competency-based assessment for individuals is described in Chapter 5, and much of that discussion applies to the identification and development of the knowledge and skills (or competencies) and behaviours that people need for effective team membership. In addition, the team itself needs to develop certain competencies or capabilities; some examples are work planning and allocation, time management, problem-solving, decision-making and the ability to focus on customer needs.

Competency-based assessment can be very valuable for assessing which of an organisation's employees have the potential to be effective members of project teams or other temporary groups. Such assessments are concerned with both an individual's technical or specialist expertise and, perhaps more importantly, that person's team behaviours and adaptability. It is another way in which individual assessments contribute to team performance.

WHO REVIEWS TEAM PERFORMANCE?

There is an obvious answer to this question: the responsibility for team performance planning and review should be the same as the responsibility for team performance management. In practice, it might be more complex than that.

Self-directed work teams are, by definition, responsible for managing their own performance. Thus, a fully empowered, mature, self-directed team will describe its own job roles, set its own standards, determine its own targets, provide its members with feedback on their work performance and team skills, review its own performance and address its members' training and development needs. This is a very optimistic prescription for most workplace teams, few of which will reach that stage of maturity.

It also tends to ignore any question about how the team and its performance are to be linked to the wider organisational system, so that the team's plans and targets are consistent with, and support achievement of, the overall mission and goals of the total organisation. As a way of monitoring this link, a team might be given responsibility for reviewing its own *working*, while the responsibility for reviewing its *work* is assigned to a performance manager outside the team. In the early stages of a team's development, the external performance manager might also be involved as a coach and facilitator who helps team members to develop effective relationships and behaviours. The performance manager gradually withdraws as the team becomes more mature and better able to deal with its own behaviours.

Many teams use self-review or self-assessment methods. Again, the choice of method should be influenced by the maturity of the team. The members of a well-established, self-directed process team might comfortably and constructively engage in open and frank discussion, but it might be better to have the participants in a temporary project team assess the contributions of their peers by anonymously filling out a standard form questionnaire. An intact team that is functioning well should be constantly checking and improving its own processes, and thus may be in the best position to provide an assessment and review. Obviously, team members are uniquely placed to assess the contributions and behaviours of other team members. In many organisations, employees have shown a real willingness to be involved in these reviews. Unfortunately, a unique perspective does not necessarily make people qualified to offer accurate or appropriate assessments and feedback, and the state of individual relationships within the team, or the stage of the team's development, might make it counterproductive for such internal assessments to be the major point of reference. And 'group think' is always a danger: the team's members might be content with the team's effectiveness, yet an impartial outside observer might take a different view.

Gathering accurate and appropriate data is as important for team performance reviews as it is for individual performance reviews. As far as performance outcomes and results are concerned, the types and sources of this information are reasonably obvious and should be readily accessible. However, different types of information will be needed to assess the team's internal processes and workings and will have different sources.

Gathering feedback from team outsiders—for example, members of other teams, other managers in the organisation, customers, suppliers—

can add to the assessments and insights of the team's behaviour. The techniques of 360-degree assessment and feedback (see Chapter 5) are easily adapted to gather this data. An example of a simple assessment questionnaire is set out in the box below.

Team performance assessment questionnaire

You are invited to contribute information that will be used in assessing the performance of members of the Alpha Project Team. Each member of the team is being asked to fill out the form—without discussing it with anyone else. The information you provide will be confidential to the team performance manager.

Please divide 100 points among all the members of the team (including yourself) according to each person's level of contribution to the project. If you think that each member contributed equally, then give each member the same number of points. You may also comment briefly on each member's contribution. Here are some criteria that you might want to consider in making your assessment:

- *Competence* — has or seeks skills and knowledge relevant to the project
- *Effort* — tries to complete assigned tasks
- *Productivity* — level of work contributed
- *Creativity* — produces useful, innovative approaches and ideas
- *Quality* — demonstrates accuracy and thoroughness
- *Dependability* — follows through on assignments and responsibilities
- *Communication* — listens and explains ideas and concepts clearly
- *Initiative* — seeks out new assignments and opportunities to contribute
- *Decision-making* — sets objectives, evaluates alternatives
- *Leadership* — fosters teamwork, helps team solve problems

Your name .... Points ....

Comments

....

....

....

....

Name of team member .... Points ....

Comments

....
....
....
....

Name of team member .... Points ....

Comments

....
....
....
....

Name of team member .... Points ....

Comments

....
....
....
....

Name of team member .... Points ....

Comments

....
....
....
....

REWARDING TEAM PERFORMANCE

If team-based working is to be taken seriously, the team should be rewarded, at least in part, as a team. Yet many organisations continue to provide team members with incentives or performance-related pay on an individual basis, or through organisation-wide schemes. As we have seen, effective team-working demands that all parts of the organisation's value systems and support structures reinforce this approach. It is weakened to the extent that the organisation continues to reward individual contributions rather than team performance. Of course, even when rewards are calculated on a team basis, they are usually distributed to the employees on an individual basis, which can further confuse the relationship of the team and its members. Some organisations solve this dilemma by distributing team-based rewards (usually in a non-cash form) only on a 'whole team' basis—so that all members of the team are invited to a celebration dinner or a weekend away at a resort, for example. Of course, if team members have different interests and lifestyles, that approach sets up other problems.

Other organisations have transformed individual pay systems into team pay systems, usually by the simple means of aggregating targets and bonus payments and sharing them equally among the members of a team. It is doubtful whether arrangements of this sort have any real effect on team performance. Skills-based pay and competencies-based pay systems (see pages 189–90) are frequently used to encourage individuals to improve the capabilities they bring to the team. Again, however, these are individual pay systems and not, in strict terms, team pay arrangements. The contrast between team pay and individual merit pay schemes is described in this way by the Institute for Employment Studies (Thompson 1995).

Team pay	Individual merit pay
• Rewards teamwork and cooperation • Encourages group to improve work systems • Increases flexibility and ability to respond to changing needs • Not incorporated in base pay • Encourages information-sharing and communication • Focus on wider organisation	• Creates internal competition • Encourages withholding of information • Individuals try to improve system—results in failure • Decreases flexibility • Incorporated into base salary • No focus on wider organisation

Clearly, it would be preferable for the pay system to be used strategically—in other words, the rewards system should be designed and developed in such a way that it would drive the move towards team-based working. In reality, adjustments to pay systems tend to come in the wake of organisational changes. Nevertheless, any organisation that plans to introduce team-based pay should start by looking closely at its readiness for this move. The questions it should ask are straightforward: What results or outcomes do we wish to encourage and reward? Are they the product of individual effort or team effort? Are the proposed team measures linked to the organisation's strategies and plans? Are we seeking to reward team work (outcomes) or team-working (process)?

Types of team rewards

Ed Lawler (1997) describes three types of team rewards.

- Individuals can be rewarded for their contributions to the team.
- The team as a whole can be rewarded for its performance.
- The team can be paid in accordance with the success of the business.

As with individual rewards, team-based rewards may be in cash or non-cash form, or a combination of the two. Many would argue that non-financial rewards are a more powerful recognition of the development and effectiveness of teamwork, and are best when derived from a supportive management and organisational culture. There are, however, many individuals and occupational groups—currency dealers and other financial services employees are a prominent example—where cash payments are important as both incentives and rewards.

For some teams, 'a carefully crafted mix of individual and group incentives may be most appropriate' (Gross 1995). The mix might be made up of the individual's base pay plus one or more of these performance-related rewards:

- **A shared team bonus.** The team's total bonus is shared equally among team members or allocated as a percentage of each individual's base salary (on the assumption that the base salary reflects the person's relative value to the team).
- **Individual competency-related pay.** This is seen as a way of rewarding the contribution that each team member is capable of making, and providing incentives to team members to develop higher levels of competency. Competency-based assessment is discussed in Chapter 5 and competency-based pay in Chapter 8.
- **Bonuses based on the performance of the organisation, department or business unit.** Gainsharing (see Chapter 8) is one team-based approach to this kind of reward.

- **Non-financial rewards**. Non-financial rewards may be intrinsic (e.g. feelings of achievement, control and worth) or extrinsic (e.g. public praise and recognition) and may, in the case of teams, be more significant than financial rewards.

The conclusion has to be that team pay, when designed and introduced carefully in the right situation, can be a powerful organisational tool. But, as Michael Armstrong (2000) says, 'it is not an easy option, and team reward processes do not run themselves—they have to be managed'.

REFERENCES

Armstrong, M 1992, *Human Resource Management: Strategy and Action*, Kogan Page, London.

Armstrong, M 1996, *Employee Reward*, Institute of Personnel and Development, London.

Armstrong, M 2000, *Rewarding Teams*, Institute of Personnel and Development, London.

Armstrong, M & Murlis, H 1991, *Reward Management*, Kogan Page, London.

Atwater, L & Waldman, D 1998, 'Accountability in 360-degree feedback', *HRMagazine*, May.

Beer, M 1984, 'Reward systems', in M Beer, B Spector, PR Lawrence, D Quinn Mills & RE Walton, *Managing Human Assets*, The Free Press, New York.

Bennis, WA 1984, 'Good managers and good leaders', *Across the Board*, October.

Bevan, S & Thompson, M 1991, 'Performance management at the crossroads', *Personnel Management*, November.

Boam, R & Sparrow, P 1992, *Designing and Achieving Competency*, McGraw-Hill, Maidenhead, England.

Borrill, CS, Carletta, J, Carter, AJ, Dawson, JF, Garrod, S, Rees, A, Richards, A, Shapiro, D & West, MA 2001, *The Effectiveness of Health Care Teams in the National Health Service*, Aston Centre for Health Service Organisational Research, Birmingham, UK.

Boyatzis, R 1982, *The Competent Manager*, Wiley, New York.

Brading, L & Wright, V 1990, 'Performance-related pay', Factsheet 30, *Personnel Management*, June.

Buckingham, M & Coffman, C 1999, *First, Break All the Rules*, Simon & Schuster, New York.

Burchman, SJ & Schneier, CE 1989, 'Assessing CEO performance', *Directors and Boards*, Winter.

Cabinet Office 2001, 'Getting the best out of 360-degree feedback', Cabinet Office, London.

Carroll, SJ, Olian, JD & Giannantonio, CM 1987, 'Performance enhancement through mentoring', in CW Schneier, RW Beatty & LS Baird (eds), *The Performance Management Sourcebook*, Human Resource Development Press, Amherst, Mass.

Carson, KP & Stewart, GL 1996, 'Job analysis and the socio-technical approach to quality: a critical examination', *Journey of Quality Management*, 1.

CCH 2000, 'Performance appraisal and management practices', *Human Resources Management*, CCH Australia Ltd, Sydney.

Conole, LJ & O'Neill, GL 1985, 'Performance management: an approach to specifying and assessing individual job performance', *Human Resource Management Australia*, 23(4).

Cooper, R 1973, 'Task characteristics and intrinsic motivation', *Human Relations*, 26.

Cross, M 1992, *Skills-based Pay: A Guide for Practitioners*, Institute of Personnel Management, London.

Deming, WE 1986, *Out of the Crisis*, MIT Institute for Advanced Engineering Study, Cambridge, Mass.

DeNisi, AS & Kluger, AN 2000, 'Feedback effectiveness: Can 360-degree appraisals be improved?' *Academy of Management Executive*, 14(1).

Drummond, H 1993, 'Measuring management effectiveness', *Personnel Management*, March.

Edwards, MR & Ewen, AJ 1996, *360° Feedback: The Powerful New Model for Employee Assessment and Performance Improvement*, AMACOM, New York.

Feltham, R 1992, 'Use of competencies in recruitment', in R Boam & P Sparrow, *Designing and Achieving Competency*, McGraw-Hill, Maidenhead, England.

Fitz-enz, J 1984, *How to Measure Human Resources Management*, McGraw-Hill, New York.

Fletcher, C 1993a, 'Appraisal: an idea whose time has gone?' *Personnel Management*, September.

Fletcher, C 1993b, *Appraisal: Routes to Improved Performance*, Institute of Personnel Management, London.

Fowler, A 1990, 'Performance management: the MBO of the '90s?' *Personnel Management*, July.

French, JRP & Raven, BH 1959, 'The bases of social power', in D Cartwright (ed.), *Studies in Social Power*, University of Michigan, Ann Arbor.

Gross, S 1995, *Compensation for Teams*, American Management Association, New York.

Guest, D 1984, 'What's new in motivation', *Personnel Management*, May.

Hackman, JR & Oldham, GR 1980, *Work Redesign*, Addison-Wesley, Reading, Mass.

Hartnett, BC 1981, 'Appraisal, bureaucracy, and industrial democracy', in RD Lansbury (ed.), *Performance Appraisal: Managing Human Resources*, Macmillan, London.

Herzberg, F 1974, 'The wise old Turk', *Harvard Business Review*, September–October.

Hornby, D & Thomas, R 1989, 'Towards a better standard of management', *Personnel Management*, January.

Institute of Personnel and Development 1996, *The IPD Policy Guide to Team Reward*, IPD, London.

Jacobs, R 1989, 'Getting the measure of managerial competence', *Personnel Management*, October.

Johnson, JW & Ferstl, KL 1999, 'The effects of inter-rater and self-other agreement on performance improvement following upward feedback', *Personnel Psychology*, 52.

Kane, JS & Lawler, EE 1978, 'Methods of peer assessment', *Psychological Bulletin*, 85.

Kanter, RM 1987, 'From status to contribution: some organisational implications of the changing basis for pay', *Personnel*, January.

Kaufman, R 1988, 'Preparing useful performance indicators', *Training and Development Journal*, September.

Kidwell, RE & Bennett, N 1993, 'Employee propensity to withhold effort: a conceptual model to intersect three avenues of research', *Academy of Management Review*, 18.

Kinnie, N & Purcell, J 1998, 'Side effects', *People Management*, 30 April.

Kohn, A 1993, 'Why incentive plans cannot work', *Harvard Business Review*, September–October.

Kotter, JP 1990, 'What leaders really do', *Harvard Business Review*, May–June.

Kovach, KA 1987, 'What motivates employees? Workers and supervisors give different answers', *Business Horizons*, September–October.

Kram, KE 1985, *Mentoring at Work: Developmental Relationships in Organisational Life*, Scott Foresman, Glenview, Ill.

Lansbury, RD 1988, 'Performance management: a process approach', *Human Resource Management Australia* 26(3).

Lansbury, RD & Prideaux, GJ 1981, 'The appraisal interview and the art of feedback' in RD Lansbury (ed.), *Performance Appraisal: Managing Human Resources*, Macmillan, London.

Latham, GP & Locke, EA 1979, 'Goal setting—a motivational technique that works', *Organisational Dynamics*, Autumn.

Lawler, EE 1997, 'Tricky but not impossible', *Across the Board*, February.

Limerick, D & Cunnington, B 1993, *Managing the New Organisation*, Business and Professional Publishing, Sydney.

Locke, EA & Latham, GP 1990, 'Work motivation and satisfaction: light at the end of the tunnel', *Psychological Science* 1(4).

London, M & Smither, JW 1995, 'Can multi-source feedback change perceptions of goal accomplishment, self-evaluations, and performance-related outcomes? Theory-based applications and directions for research', *Personnel Psychology*, 48.

Maier, NRF 1976, *The Appraisal Interview: Three Basic Approaches*, University Associates, La Jolla, Cal.

Matell, MS & Jacoby, J 1972, 'Is there an optimal number of alternatives for Likert-style items?' *Journal of Applied Psychology*, 56.

Mayfield, H 1960, 'In defense of performance appraisal', *Harvard Business Review*, March–April.

McClelland, DC 1967, 'Money as a motivator: some research insights', *The McKinsey Quarterly*.

McClelland, DC 1970, 'The two faces of power', *Journal of International Affairs*, 24(1).

McGregor, D 1957, 'An uneasy look at performance appraisal', *Harvard Business Review*, May–June.

McGuire, PJ 1980, 'Why performance appraisals fail', *Personnel Journal*, September.

Meyer, HH 1980, 'Self-appraisal of job performance', *Personnel Psychology*, 33.

Meyer, HH, Kay, E & French, JRP 1965, 'Split roles in performance appraisal', *Harvard Business Review*, January.

Morgan, RB & Smith, JE 1996, *Staffing the New Workplace: Selecting and Promoting for Quality Improvement*, ASQC Press, Milwaukee.

Mumford, A 1993, 'How managers can become developers', *Personnel Management*, June.

Peters, T 1994, *The pursuit of WOW!* Vintage Books, New York.

Porter, LW, Lawler, EE & Hackman, JR 1975, *Behavior in Organizations*, McGraw-Hill, New York.

Purcell, J 2000, 'Pay per view', *People Management*, 3 February.

Randell, G 1989, 'A rejoinder to Handy: is it what you are or what you do?' *The Occupational Psychologist*, December.

Raven, BH & Kruglanski, W 1975, 'Conflict and power', in PG Swingle (ed.), *The Structure of Conflict*, Academic Press, New York.

Rummler, GA 1972, 'Human performance problems and their solutions', *Human Resource Management*, Winter.

Sahl, R 1998, 'Good teams or good performance? Issues in developing team-based measurements', *Journal of Compensation and Benefits*, January–February, 13(4).

Sala, F & Dwight, S 2002, 'Predicting executive performance with multi-rater surveys: who you ask matters', Paper for SIOP Conference 2002, http://ei.haygroup.com/resources/Library_articles/Predicting.Exec.Perf.doc [23 October 2002].

Sashkin, M 1981, *Assessing Performance Appraisal*, University Associates Inc, San Diego.

Schneier, CE & Beatty, EW 1979, 'Developing BARS', *Personnel Administrator*, August.

Scott, SG & Einstein, WO 2001, 'Strategic performance appraisal in team-based organisations: one size does not fit all', *Academy of Management Executive*, 15(2).

SHRM/PDI 2000, *Performance Management Survey*, Society for Human

Resource Management/Personnel Decisions International, Washington DC.

Singer, EJ 1979, *Effective Management Coaching*, Institute of Personnel Management, London.

Slater, JA & West, MA 1995, 'Satisfaction or source of pressure: the paradox of teamwork', *The Occupational Psychologist*, April.

Strebler, MT, Bevan, S & Robinson, D 2001, *Performance Review: Balancing Objectives and Content*, Report 370, Institute for Employment Studies, London.

Thompson, M 1992, *Pay and Performance: The Employee Experience*, Institute of Manpower Studies, London.

Thompson, M 1995, *Team Working and Pay*, IES Report No 281, Institute for Employment Studies, London.

Townley, B 1990, 'A discriminating approach to appraisal', *Personnel Management*, December.

Turner, AN & Lawrence, PR 1965, *Industrial Jobs and the Worker: An Investigation of Response to Task Attributes*, Harvard University, Boston, Mass.

Ungerson, B 1983, *How to Write a Job Description*, Institute of Personnel Management, London.

United States Office of Personnel Management 1998, *Performance Appraisal for Teams: An Overview*, Washington, DC.

Walker, A & Smither, J 1999, 'A five-year study of upward feedback: what managers do with their results matters', *Personnel Psychology*, 52(2).

Ward, P 1997, *360-degree Feedback*, Institute of Personnel and Development, London.

Wexley, KN & Klimowski, R 1984, 'Performance appraisal: an update', in KM Rowland & GD Ferris (eds), *Research in Personnel and Human Resources*, JAI Press, Greenwich, CT.

Woodruffe, C 1990, *Assessment Centres: Identifying and Developing Competencies*, Institute of Personnel Management, London.

Wright, V 1991, 'Performance-related pay', in F Neale (ed.), *The Handbook of Performance Management*, Institute of Personnel Management, London.

INDEX

accountability
  and knowledge workers
    18
  and managers 60–5
adult learning 152
alternation ranking 71–2
appraisal of planning and
  review 3, 4, 22
appraisal methods 68–98
arguing in performance
  discussions 132
Armstrong, M. 9, 191, 210
attributional error 100–1
Atwater, L. and Waldman, D.
  107

Beer, M. 175
Behaviourally Anchored
  Rating Scales (BARS) 67,
  68, 83–5
Behavioural criteria 92–3
Behavioural Observation
  Scales (BOS) 86–8
Bennis, W. A. 145
Bevan, S. and Thompson, M.
  22, 174
bias 37, 100
Boam, R. and Sparrow, R. 94
body language 110, 129
bonus schemes 183–4, 188,
  209
Borrill, C.S. et al. 2
Boyatzis, R. 94
Brading, L. and Wright, V.
  173
Buckingham, M. and
  Coffman, C. 145
Burchman, S. J. and Schneier,
  C. E. 61

career advancement pay 191
CCH Australia 22, 26
Cabinet Office (UK) 108
career development and
  planning 46, 159–60,
  169–72
career development pay 191
Carroll, S. J., Olian, J. D. and
  Giannantonio, C. M. 157
Carson, K. P. and Stewart,
  G. L. 47

central tendency error 79, 99
checklists 73, 75–6
closed questions 127
coaching 147, 153–9
communication skills 41–2,
  113–14, 126–33
communication styles
  one-way communication
    123
comparison methods 70–3
competency analysis 94–8
competency-based assessment
  33, 67, 93–8
competencies-based pay 190,
  208, 209
conflicts in performance
  planning and review 26–8,
  117
Conole, L. J. and O'Neill,
  G. L. 9
constructive criticism 66
contingent working 5, 14
contrast error 100
Cooper, R. 14
counselling 132
critical incidents 73, 74–5
criticism in performance
  discussions 66, 131–2
Cross, M. 190
cultural factors 2, 130

Deming, W. E. 1, 20, 43, 55,
  62–3
DeNisi, A. S. and Kluger,
  A. N. 107
desirability index 76
directive interview 118
discrimination in performance reviews 69
discrimination index 76
Drucker, P. F. 89
Drummond, H. 63

Edwards, M. R. and Ewen,
  A. J. 106
Einstein, A. 43
employee shareholding
  188–9
Enron Corporation 73
equity theory 177
errors in performance review

79, 98–101, 103
essays 74
example of performance
  planning and review
  format 133–43
expectancy theory 173,
  177–8

feedback 28, 38, 130–1,
  150–1
  and coaching 157–8
  effective feedback 130
  methods compared 106
  360-degree feedback
    106–13
Feltham, R. 95
first impression error 99–100
Fitz-enz, J. 54
Fletcher, C. 1, 101, 102
flexible working arrange-
  ments 5, 13–14
forced choice 73, 76
forced distribution 68
Ford Motor Company 73
forms 36–7, 42, 89, 126,
  133–43
Fowler, A. 23
French, J. R. P. and Raven,
  B. H. 147

gain sharing 188
Gallup Organisation 145
General Electric Company
  31
Glaxo Wellcome 16
goals 42, 51–2
  see also targets
  goal setting 55–6, 105
  for managers 33
graphic rating scales 76, 78
Gross, S. 209
Guest, D. 178

Hackman, J. R. and Oldham,
  G. R. 15
halo effect 79, 99
harshness error 99
Hartnett, B. C. 122
Herzberg, F. 15, 176
Hornby, D. and Thomas, R.
  94

horns effect 99
Humble, J. 89

incentive schemes 173, 183–4
individuals cf. teams 13, 15, 16, 193–5, 198–200
Institute for Employment Studies 208
Institute of Manpower Studies 174, 182
Institute of Personnel and Development 192
International Labour Office 173

Jacobs, R. 94
job analysis 45, 46, 95
job descriptions 45–51
for managers
job design 13–15, 45
job evaluation 45, 46
Johnson, J. W. and Ferstl, K. L. 105

Kane, J. S. and Lawler, E. E. 104
Kanter, R. M. 188
Kaufman, R. 53
key results areas 52
Kidwell, R. E. and Bennett, N. 198
Kinnie, N. and Purcell, J. 193
knowledge-based pay 189–190
knowledge workers 16–20
Kohn, A. 182
Kotter, J. P. 145
Kovach, K. A. 176
Kram, K. E. 156

Lansbury, R. D. 9
Lansbury, R. D. and Prideaux, G. J. 130
Latham, G. P. and Locke, E. A. 56
Lawler, E. E. 209
leadership 145–6
learning organisation 144
learning process 147–52
leniency error 99, 103
Limerick, D. 195
linear rating scales 76
listening 128–9
Locke, E. A. and Latham, G. P. 105
logical error 100
London, M. and Smither, J. W. 107

Maier, N. R. F. 103, 116, 118
manager's role 7, 8, 10, 12, 27, 32, 39, 145–7
Management by Objectives (MBO) 8, 23, 59, 89–92
management competences 95–8
management defined 8
Matell, M. S. and Jacoby, J. 77
Mayfield, H. 4
Mayo, E. 177
McClelland, D. C. 147, 177
McGregor, D. 24, 39
McGuire, P. J. 29
measurement 42, 51–5, 54–5, 57
mentoring 156–7
merit pay 179, 182–3, 188
Meyer, H. H. 180
Meyer, H. H., Kay, E. and French, J. R. P. 31
model format
performance planning and review 133–43
performance development 161–6
Morgan, R. B. and Smith, J. E. 47
multi-rater assessment 106
multi-source feedback 106
Mumford, A. 154

narrative appraisals 74
'new' employees 16–20
non-directive interview 118
note-taking in performance discussions 132–3

objections to performance planning and review 40–4
objectives of performance planning and review 24–6, 28, 39
objectivity in performance review 68
Office of Personnel Management (US) 195–6, 199–200
open questions 126–7

paired comparisons 68–9, 72
Payment By Results (PBR) 173
pay for competencies 190
pay for skills/knowledge 189–90
paying for team performance 191–2
peer assessment or review 18, 101, 104

performance
defined 7
planning 10, 45–65
targets see targets
performance appraisal
arguments for 1–2
criticisms 1, 5, 20
impact 2
objectives 4, 24
role 2
term 3, 34
use of 2
performance development 25, 27, 32, 144–72
performance development discussion 159–66
review example 161–6
performance discussion or interview 38, 80, 115–43
arrangements 120–2
communication 123, preparation 38, 103, 119–20
purpose 115–18
structure 122–6
style 116–17, 123
performance indicators 53–4
performance management 8–21
definition 9, 10, features 10, 22–3, 31–2
objectives 9
process cf. people approach 23
performance measures 53–5, 57
teams 200–4
performance pay 8, 36, 173–5, 180–9
criticisms 182
features 181
types 182–8
performance planning and review
definition 3, 24–5, objectives 24–26, 28, 39
part of a process 34–5
and performance management 4
and performance development 32
and remuneration 36, 118
teams 193–210
timing 35–6, 38
performance problems 166–9
guidelines for handling 168–9
performance ratings 81–2
performance review 10, 27, 66–114

guidelines 67, 120
teams 200–7
training 113–14, 120
performance–rewards
exchange 175–7
performance standards 33,
42, 49, 51–5
person profiles 46, 48
personal development 25
personality 37, 43
Peters, T. 1
prejudice 100
planning performance 10,
45–65
power and authority 146–7
problem employees 166–7
process teams 196, 203
professional employees *see*
knowledge workers
profit sharing 188–9
project teams 196–7, 203
Purcell, J. 174

questionnaire, 360-degree
feedback 110–12
questions in the performance
discussion 126–8

Randell, G. 94, 160
ranking methods 68, 70–3
problems 70–1
rating scales 74, 76–88
problems 77–9
Raven, B. H. and Kruglanski,
W. 147
recency error 99–100
reliability 70
remuneration
link to performance review
36, 118, 178–81
results-oriented reviews 88–93
problems 90–2
review methods 68–98
alternation ranking 71–2
BARS 83–5
Behavioural Observation
Scales (BOS) 86–8
checklists 73, 75
comparison methods 70–3

competency based assess-
ment 93–8
critical incidents 73, 74–5
essays 74
external reviewers 113
forced choice 73, 75
forced distribution 68, 72
Management by Objectives
89–92
narrative appraisals 74
paired comparisons 72
peer reviews 104
rating scales 74, 76–88
results oriented reviews
88–93
ranking methods 70–3
rating scales 74
self-assessment 102–4
standards based reviews
73–88
straight ranking 71
teams 200–7
upwards appraisal 38
reviewer, selection of 101–6
reviewing performance
66–114
rewarding performance
173–92
team rewards 207–10
rewards and recognition
148–9, 175–7
reward punishment
psychology 150–1
Rummler, G. A. 168–9

Sahl, R. 201
Sala, F. and Dwight, S. 109
Sashkin, M. 31
Schneier, C. E. and Beatty,
E. W. 83
Scott, S. G. and Einstein,
W. O. 197
self-assessment 102–4
similarity/dissimilarity error
99
Singer, E. 154
skewed distribution 79
skills-based pay 189–90, 208
Slater, J. A. and West,
M. A. 195

social loafing 197
Society for Human Resource
Management 145
standards-based reviews
73–88
standards 52–3
straight ranking 71
Strebler, M. T., Bevan, S. and
Robinson, D. 2, 31
subordinates, review by
105–6
succession planning 46
Sun Microsystems 73

targets 51–65
see also goals
for managers 60–5
SMART targets 56–60
and motivation 55–6
team rewards 191–2, 207–10
team-working 5, 13, 15,
193–5
and performance manage-
ment 15–16
and performance planning
and review 193–210
Thompson, M. 174, 182,
208
360-degree feedback 106–13
timing 35–6, 38
Townley, B. 69
training 147–8
Turner, A. N. and Lawrence,
P. R. 14

Ungerson, B. 48
upwards review or feedback
38, 105–6

validity 70

Walker, A. and Smither,
J. 105
Ward, P. 109, 110
West, M. 2
Wexley, K. N. and
Klimowski, R. 77
Woodruffe, C. 93, 94
Wright, V. 180

DATE DUE

#47-0108 Peel Off Pressure Sensitive